Medical Rights

Other Books in the Issues on Trial Series:

Medical Rights

Sylvia Engdahl, Book Editor

GREENHAVEN PRESS
A part of Gale, Cengage Learning

GALE
CENGAGE Learning™

Detroit • New York • San Francisco • New Haven, Conn • Waterville, Maine • London

GALE
CENGAGE Learning

Christine Nasso, *Publisher*
Elizabeth Des Chenes, *Managing Editor*

© 2009 Greenhaven Press, a part of Gale, Cengage Learning

For more information, contact:
Greenhaven Press
27500 Drake Rd.
Farmington Hills, MI 48331-3535
Or you can visit our Internet site at gale.cengage.com.

For product information and technology assistance, contact us at

Gale Customer Support, 1-800-877-4253
For permission to use material from this text or product, submit all requests online at www.cengage.com/permissions

Further permissions questions can be emailed to permissionrequest@cengage.com

Articles in Greenhaven Press anthologies are often edited for length to meet page requirements. In addition, original titles of these works are changed to clearly present the main thesis and to explicitly indicate the author's opinion. Every effort is made to ensure that Greenhaven Press accurately reflects the original intent of the authors. Every effort has been made to trace the owners of copyrighted material.

Cover photograph reproduced by permission of © Robert Maass/Corbis.

LIBRARY OF CONGRESS CATALOGING-IN-PUBLICATION DATA

Medical rights / Sylvia Engdahl, book editor.
    p. cm. -- (Issues on trial)
   Includes bibliographical references and index.
   ISBN-13: 978-0-7377-4179-7 (hardcover)
   1. Medical laws and legislation--United States--Cases. I. Engdahl, Sylvia. II. Series.
   KF3821.M398 2009
   344.7304'1--dc22

                         2008028527

Printed in the United States of America
1 2 3 4 5 6 7 12 11 10 09 08

Contents

Chapter 2: Affirming the Right of Competent Adults to Refuse Medical Treatment

Chapter 3: Establishing the Right of Mentally Ill Defendants to Refuse Medication

Chapter 4: Denying the Right of Terminally Ill Persons to Use Experimental Drugs

Foreword

The U.S. courts have long served as a battleground for the most highly charged and contentious issues of the time. Divisive matters are often brought into the legal system by activists who feel strongly for their cause and demand an official resolution. Indeed, subjects that give rise to intense emotions or involve closely held religious or moral beliefs lay at the heart of the most polemical court rulings in history. One such case was *Brown v. Board of Education* (1954), which ended racial segregation in schools. Prior to *Brown*, the courts had held that blacks could be forced to use separate facilities as long as these facilities were equal to that of whites.

For years many groups had opposed segregation based on religious, moral, and legal grounds. Educators produced heartfelt testimony that segregated schooling greatly disadvantaged black children. They noted that in comparison to whites, blacks received a substandard education in deplorable conditions. Religious leaders such as Martin Luther King Jr. preached that the harsh treatment of blacks was immoral and unjust. Many involved in civil rights law, such as Thurgood Marshall, called for equal protection of all people under the law, as their study of the Constitution had indicated that segregation was illegal and un-American. Whatever their motivation for ending the practice, and despite the threats they received from segregationists, these ardent activists remained unwavering in their cause.

Those fighting against the integration of schools were mainly white southerners who did not believe that whites and blacks should intermingle. Blacks were subordinate to whites, they maintained, and society had to resist any attempt to break down strict color lines. Some white southerners charged that segregated schooling was *not* hindering blacks' education. For example, Virginia attorney general J. Lindsay Almond asserted, "With the help and the sympathy and the love and respect of the white people of the South, the colored man has risen under that educational process to a place of eminence and respect throughout the nation. It has served him well." So when the Supreme Court ruled against the segregationists in *Brown*, the South responded with vociferous cries of protest. Even government leaders criticized the decision. The governor of Arkansas, Orval Faubus, stated that he would not "be a party to any attempt to force acceptance of change to which the people are so overwhelmingly opposed." Indeed, resistance to integration was so great that when black students arrived at the formerly all-white Central High School in Arkansas, federal troops had to be dispatched to quell a threatening mob of protesters.

Nevertheless, the *Brown* decision was enforced and the South integrated its schools. In this instance, the Court, while not settling the issue to everyone's satisfaction, functioned as an instrument of progress by forcing a major social change. Historian David Halberstam observes that the *Brown* ruling "deprived segregationist practices of their moral legitimacy. . . . It was therefore perhaps the single most important moment of the decade, the moment that separated the old order from the new and helped create the tumultuous era just arriving." Considered one of the most important victories for civil rights, *Brown* paved the way for challenges to racial segregation in many areas, including on public buses and in restaurants.

In examining *Brown*, it becomes apparent that the courts play an influential role—and face an arduous challenge—in shaping the debate over emotionally charged social issues. Judges must balance competing interests, keeping in mind the high stakes and intense emotions on both sides. As exemplified by *Brown*, judicial decisions often upset the status quo and initiate significant changes in society. Greenhaven Press's Issues on Trial series captures the controversy surrounding influential court rulings and explores the social ramifications of such decisions from varying perspectives. Each anthology highlights one social issue—such as the death penalty, students' rights, or wartime civil liberties. Each volume then focuses on key historical and contemporary court cases that helped mold the issue as we know it today. The books include a compendium of primary sources—court rulings, dissents, and immediate reactions to the rulings—as well as secondary sources from experts in the field, people involved in the cases, legal analysts, and other commentators opining on the implications and legacy of the chosen cases. An annotated table of contents, an in-depth introduction, and prefaces that overview each case all provide context as readers delve into the topic at hand. To help students fully probe the subject, each volume contains book and periodical bibliographies, a comprehensive index, and a list of organizations to contact. With these features, the Issues on Trial series offers a well-rounded perspective on the courts' role in framing society's thorniest, most impassioned debates.

Introduction

The term "medical rights" is often used to refer to all the rights patients have in their relationships with doctors and hospitals, or to the belief of some people that everyone has a right to receive medical care regardless of its cost. This is not the sense, however, in which it is used in connection with Supreme Court cases. The Supreme Court is concerned with constitutional rights: principles expressed in the U.S. Constitution, such as the right to equal protection under the law and the rights to liberty and privacy. It also makes judgments about what federal laws require in particular circumstances. When a case involving medical issues comes before the Court, the only thing to be decided is what bearing the Constitution or a federal law has on those issues.

This is not to say that the justices (judges) of the Court do not consider moral and social aspects of the case in presenting their opinions, for they often do. It is the role of the Supreme Court to interpret the Constitution—that is, to decide what its statements mean in the practical sense. Frequently, its members do not agree about the meaning; that is why most cases are decided on the basis of a majority vote. In general, some Supreme Court justices believe in a strict interpretation of the Constitution according to what it meant to its authors at the time it was written, while others believe that it should be interpreted in the light of modern conditions. This conflict is particularly relevant to decisions concerning medical issues because most such issues have arisen comparatively recently.

Relatively few cases involving medical issues have reached the Supreme Court, although many have been decided in the lower courts. The majority of those that the Supreme Court has reviewed have concerned reproductive rights, the question of abortion, or physician-assisted suicide—topics that are covered by other books in the *Issues on Trial* series. This book deals with different sorts of cases.

Usually, the conflict in a Supreme Court case is between a state or federal authority and an individual—or group of individuals—who believe the law or practice in question violates their rights. The Court has the power to overrule state and federal laws on the grounds that they are unconstitutional and therefore invalid. The legal system, however, does not allow anyone to simply assert that a law or regulation is unfair. To bring a suit before the Supreme Court (or any federal court), a person or group must have "standing," which means they must personally have been harmed, or will actually—not merely hypothetically—be harmed in the future. Therefore, every case that the Court considers involves a real individual whose life has been affected by a specific problem.

The cases described in this book, for example, include those of Henning Jacobson, who was jailed for refusing to be vaccinated against smallpox; Nancy Cruzan, who was being kept artificially alive in a hospital against her expressed wish although she could never regain consciousness; Charles Sell, who resisted being given psychiatric drugs by force to enable him to stand trial for fraud; and Abigail Burroughs, who died after the law prevented her from obtaining new experimental drugs to fight cancer. If their personal stories were all that the Court had to consider, it might look as if it would be simple to decide their cases in their favor. But it is much more complicated than that. Every law affects more than one individual. So the question is not just whether the individual who brought suit has been harmed—which was a requirement for filing suit in the first place—but whether, under the Constitution, that harm was more serious than the problems or potential problems that the law was designed to prevent.

Sometimes, however, there is no need for such balancing, and the Court simply decides whether or not the person's problem was the result of constitutional rights being misunderstood or ignored. For instance, while there is nothing in the Constitution that gives everyone the right to receive medical care, in 1976 the Supreme Court ruled that inmates of prisons do have such a right because to deprive them of medical care would constitute "cruel and unusual punishment," which is forbidden by the Constitution's Eighth Amendment.

In that case, *Estelle v. Gamble*, an inmate named J. W. Gamble was injured when a bale of cotton fell on him while he was unloading a truck as part of a prison work assignment. He was sent to a doctor, who prescribed pain pills and gave him a pass allowing him to remain in his cell. But after several weeks, although his pain was no better, the doctor said Gamble could return to work, and he was disciplined when he refused to do so. When he was examined by another doctor, the prescription that doctor gave him was not filled for some days because the prison staff lost it. Over a period of two months, he developed severe headaches in addition to his back pain, eventually being placed in solitary confinement because the doctors who saw him said he was fit to work. Finally, when he complained of chest pains and blackouts, still another doctor hospitalized him and treated him for an irregular heart rhythm; however, the guards refused when he asked to see that doctor again. By this time, two months had passed since his original injury.

Gamble swore out a complaint stating that prison officials had subjected him to cruel and unusual punishment in violation of the Eighth Amendment. The circuit court agreed that not enough had been done to diagnose his pain, saying that his back should have been X-rayed. The Supreme Court, however, ruled against him on the grounds that the failure of the doctors who saw him to perform enough diagnostic procedures was merely medical malpractice, not punishment, and that they could be sued for malpractice in state court. Although in this particular case the petitioner lost, the written opinion of Court had far-reaching effects. In it, Justice Thurgood Marshall established the precedent giving constitutional status to the medical rights of prisoners.

"An inmate must rely on prison authorities to treat his medical needs," Justice Marshall wrote. "If the authorities fail to do so, those needs will not be met. . . . Denial of medical care may result in pain and suffering which no one suggests would serve any penological purpose. The infliction of such unnecessary suffering is inconsistent with contemporary standards of decency. . . . We therefore conclude that deliberate indifference to serious medical needs of prisoners constitutes the 'unnecessary and wanton infliction of pain' proscribed by the Eighth Amendment."

What the Supreme Court says in its majority opinions about specific cases is legally applicable to all future cases that involve the same issue. It is binding on lower courts unless overruled in a later Supreme Court opinion, and the Court does not overrule itself without an exceptionally good reason. Therefore, whereas each case begins with an account of what has happened to one particular person or group, its outcome affects large numbers of people from that time on. All of today's opponents of vaccination are affected by the opinion the Court issued when it decided over a hundred years ago that Henning Jacobson could not avoid a penalty for refusing to be vaccinated. All prisoners today are affected by the chain of events that began when J. W. Gamble was injured while unloading a truck. This is the reason why the Court's opinions are important to everyone.

CHAPTER 1

Denying Adults the Right to Refuse to Comply with Public Health Laws

Case Overview

Henning Jacobson v. Commonwealth of Massachusetts (1905)

Over one hundred years ago, a man named Henning Jacobson, in defiance of Massachusetts state law, refused to be vaccinated against smallpox. He pleaded not guilty on the grounds that he believed the law was contrary to the spirit of the U.S. Constitution and it violated the Fourteenth Amendment to the U.S. Constitution, under which no state can make or enforce any law abridging the privileges or immunities of citizens of the United States. The judge disagreed and instructed the jury that if they were satisfied beyond a reasonable doubt that he had broken the law, they should find him guilty. After they did so, Jacobson took his case to the state supreme court, which upheld the trial court and ordered him to pay a fine of $5. Since he was unwilling to pay, he was put in jail, whereupon he appealed to the U.S. Supreme Court. Although at that time $5 was a more significant amount of money than it is now, his aim in fighting his conviction was less a matter of money than of principle.

In 1905, the Supreme Court ruled 7–2 against Jacobson, stating that laws requiring vaccination are not unconstitutional. (The dissenting justices did not issue written opinions.) A community is entitled to protect itself against disease, said the Court, and individual liberty does not outweigh public safety. Moreover, Jacobson's arguments against established beliefs about vaccination were based on theory rather than evidence. If they were a sufficient reason to exempt him, then vaccination laws could not be legally enforced anywhere, under any conditions; and the Court felt that it should not "invade the domain of local authority." Once the Supreme Court has made a decision in a case, it remains in force unless the

Court modifies it by a ruling in a later case. So *Jacobson* is still the legal basis of compulsory vaccination today.

Vaccination has been a controversial issue ever since the first laws requiring it were passed in the nineteenth century. Although almost all doctors and the majority of Americans have believed—and still believe—that it is necessary to prevent epidemics, a vocal minority has always been opposed to it. Jacobson's declaration that "a compulsory vaccination law is unreasonable, arbitrary, and oppressive, and, therefore, hostile to the inherent right of every freeman to care for his own body and health in such way as to him seems best" sounds very much like the arguments of modern protestors. Nevertheless, despite an ever-increasing concern for the constitutional rights of individual citizens, the law does not view vaccination requirements as a violation of those rights. Vaccination against smallpox is no longer required because smallpox, which was prevalent and serious in Jacobson's time, has been wiped out; but new kinds of vaccination have taken its place.

While in *Jacobson* the Supreme Court upheld the use of police power for community welfare, it also placed limits on that power—limits that have shaped public health law ever since. The majority opinion made clear that such laws are constitutional only when they are necessary to protect the health or safety of the public. The method employed must be reasonable, and must have a "real or substantial" relationship to public protection. Health regulations may not be arbitrary or oppressive. Finally, they must not cause direct harm to the person to whom they apply. *Jacobson* was the first Supreme Court analysis of the balance between individual rights and the public good. Because of the standards it defined, some commentators view the decision not as a restriction of liberty, but as a means of ensuring it.

> *"In every well-ordered society ... the
> rights of the individual in respect of his
> liberty may at times, under the pres-
> sure of great dangers, be subjected to
> such restraint, to be enforced by rea-
> sonable regulations, as the safety of the
> general public may demand."*

The Court's Decision: Public Health Considerations Outweigh the Right to Personal Liberty

John Marshall Harlan

*John Marshall Harlan was a justice of the U.S. Supreme Court
between 1877 and 1911. He was known as "the great dissenter"
because he often disagreed with the Court majority. His most famous dissent was in the* Plessy v. Ferguson *(1896) case, in
which the majority held that racial segregation—then commonly
practiced in the southern states—was constitutional. His opinion
in this case, however, represents the majority. In it, he explains
why the Court has decided that local authorities have the right
to require vaccination by law and why the defendant, Henning
Jacobson, has no constitutional grounds for claiming exemption
from that law. A community has the right to protect itself from
disease, he says, and the wishes of a minority cannot defy the
will of the majority. Furthermore, although Jacobson argued that*

John Marshall Harlan, majority opinion, *Henning Jacobson v. Commonwealth of Massachusetts*, U.S. Supreme Court, February 20, 1905.

vaccination is sometimes harmful and that he had been made ill by it as a child, he presented no evidence that it would still be harmful to him.

We come, . . . to inquire whether any right given or secured by the Constitution is invaded by the statute as interpreted by the state court. The defendant insists that his liberty is invaded when the state subjects him to fine or imprisonment for neglecting or refusing to submit to vaccination; that a compulsory vaccination law is unreasonable, arbitrary, and oppressive, and, therefore, hostile to the inherent right of every freeman to care for his own body and health in such way as to him seems best; and that the execution of such a law against one who objects to vaccination, no matter for what reason, is nothing short of an assault upon his person. But the liberty secured by the Constitution of the United States to every person within its jurisdiction does not import an absolute right in each person to be, at all times and in all circumstances, wholly freed from restraint. There are manifold restraints to which every person is necessarily subject for the common good. On any other basis organized society could not exist with safety to its members. Society based on the rule that each one is a law unto himself would soon be confronted with disorder and anarchy. Real liberty for all could not exist under the operation of a principle which recognizes the right of each individual person to use his own, whether in respect of his person or his property, regardless of the injury that may be done to others. This court has more than once recognized it as a fundamental principle that "persons and property are subjected to all kinds of restraints and burdens in order to secure the general comfort, health, and prosperity of the state; of the perfect right of the legislature to do which no question ever was, or upon acknowledged general principles ever can be, made, so far as natural persons are concerned" (*Hannibal & St. J. R. Co. v. Husen*). In *Crowley v. Christensen*, we said: "The possession and enjoyment of all rights are subject to such reasonable conditions as may be deemed by the governing authority of the country essential to the safety, health, peace, good order, and morals of the community. Even liberty itself, the greatest of all rights, is not unrestricted license to act according to one's own will. It is only freedom from restraint under conditions essential to the equal enjoyment of the same right by others. It is, then, liberty regulated by law...."

A Community Has the Right to Protect Itself

Applying these principles to the present case, it is to be observed that the legislature of Massachusetts required the inhabitants of a city or town to be vaccinated only when, in the opinion of the board of health, that was necessary for the public health or the public safety.... Upon the principle of self-defense, of paramount necessity, a community has the right to protect itself against an epidemic of disease which threatens the safety of its members. It is to be observed that when the regulation in question was adopted smallpox, according to the recitals in the regulation adopted by the board of health, was prevalent to some extent in the city of Cambridge, and the disease was increasing. If such was the situation—and nothing is asserted or appears in the record to the contrary—if we are to attach, any value whatever to the knowledge which, it is safe to affirm, in common to all civilized peoples touching smallpox and the methods most usually employed to eradicate that disease, it cannot be adjudged that the present regulation of the board of health was not necessary in order to protect the public health and secure the public safety. Smallpox being prevalent and increasing at Cambridge, the court would usurp the functions of another branch of government if it adjudged, as matter of law, that the mode adopted under the sanction of the state, to protect the people at large was arbitrary, and not justified by the necessities of the case.... If the mode adopted by the commonwealth of Massachusetts for the protection of its local communities against smallpox proved to be distressing, inconvenient, or objectionable to some—if nothing more could be reasonably affirmed of the statute in question—the answer is that it was the duty of the constituted authorities primarily to keep in view the welfare, comfort, and safety of the many, and not permit the interests of the many to be subordinated to the wishes or convenience of the few. There is, of course, a sphere within which the individual may assert the supremacy of his own will, and rightfully dispute the authority of any human government— especially of any free government existing under a written constitution, to interfere with the exercise of that will. But it is equally true that in every well-ordered society charged with the duty of conserving the safety of its members the rights of the individual in respect of his liberty may at times, under the pressure of great dangers, be subjected to such restraint to be enforced by reasonable regulations, as the safety of the general public may demand. An American citizen arriving at an American port on a vessel in which, during the voyage, there had been cases of yellow fever or Asiatic cholera, he, although apparently free from disease himself, may yet, in some circumstances, be held in quarantine against his will on board of such vessel or in a quarantine station, until it be ascertained by inspection, conducted with due diligence, that the danger of the spread of the disease among the community at large has disappeared. The liberty secured by the 14th Amendment, this court has said, consists, in part, in the right of a person "to live and work where he will" (*Allgeyer v. Louisiana*); and yet he may be compelled, by force if need be, against his will and without regard to his personal wishes or his pecuniary interests, or even his religious or political convictions, to take his place in the ranks of the army of his country, and risk the chance of being shot down in its defense. It is not, therefore, true that the power of the public to guard itself against imminent danger depends in every case involving the control of one's body upon his willingness to submit to reasonable regulations established by the constituted authorities, under the sanction of the state, for the purpose of protecting the public collectively against such danger.

It is said, however, that the statute, as interpreted by the state court, although making an exception in favor of children certified by a registered physician to be unfit subjects for vaccination, makes no exception in case of adults in like condition. But this cannot be deemed a denial of the equal protection of the laws to adults; for the statute is applicable equally to all in like condition, and there are obviously reasons why regulations may be appropriate for adults which could not be safely applied to persons of tender years.

The Defendant's Arguments Are Not Valid

Looking at the propositions embodied in the defendant's rejected offers to proof, it is clear that they are more formidable by their number than by their inherent value. Those offers in the main seem to have had no purpose except to state the general theory of those of the medical profession who attach little or no value to vaccination as a means of preventing the spread of smallpox, or who think that vaccination causes other diseases of the body. What everybody knows the court must know, and therefore the state court judicially knew, as this court knows, that an opposite theory accords with the common belief, and is maintained by high medical authority. We must assume that, when the statute in question was passed, the legislature of Massachusetts was not unaware of these opposing theories, and was compelled, of necessity, to choose between them. It was not compelled to commit a matter involving the public health and safety to the final decision of a court or jury. It is no part of the function of a court or a jury to determine which one of two modes was likely to be the most effective for the protection of the public against disease.

That was for the legislative department to determine in the light of all the information it had or could obtain. It could not properly abdicate its function to guard the public health and safety. The state legislature proceeded upon the theory which recognized vaccination as at least an effective, if not the best-known, way in which to meet and suppress the evils of a smallpox epidemic that imperiled an entire population. . . .

Whatever may be thought of the expediency of this statute, it cannot be affirmed to be, beyond question, in palpable conflict with the Constitution. Nor, in view of the methods employed to stamp out the disease of smallpox, can anyone confidently assert that the means prescribed by the state to that end has no real or substantial relation to the protection of the public health and the public safety. Such an assertion would not be consistent with the experience of this and other countries whose authorities have dealt with the disease of smallpox. And the principle of vaccination as a means to prevent the spread of smallpox has been enforced in many states by statutes making the vaccination of children a condition of their right to enter or remain in public schools. The latest case upon the subject of which we are aware is *Viemester v. White*, decided very recently by the court of appeals of New York. That case involved the validity of a statute excluding from the public schools all children who had not been vaccinated.

One contention was that the statute and the regulation adopted in exercise of its provisions was inconsistent with the rights, privileges, and liberties of the citizen. The contention was overruled, the court saying, among other things: "Smallpox is known of all to be a dangerous and contagious disease. If vaccination strongly tends to prevent the transmission or spread of this disease, it logically follows that children may be refused admission to the public schools until they have been vaccinated. The appellant claims that vaccination does not tend to prevent smallpox, but tends to bring about other diseases, and that it does much harm, with no good. It must be conceded that some laymen, both learned and unlearned, and some physicians of great skill and repute, do not believe that vaccination is a preventive of smallpox. The common belief, however, is that it has a decided tendency to prevent the spread of this fearful disease, and to render it less dangerous to those who contract it. While not accepted by all, it is accepted by the mass of the people, as well as by most members of the medical profession. It has been general in our state, and in most civilized nations for generations. It is generally accepted in theory, and generally applied in practice, both by the voluntary action of the people, and in obedience to the command of law. Nearly every state in the Union has statutes to encourage, or directly or indirectly to require, vaccination; and this is true of most nations of Europe. . . . A common belief, like common knowledge, does not require evidence to establish its existence, but may be acted upon without proof by the legislature and the courts. . . . The fact that the belief is not universal is not controlling, for there is scarcely any belief that is accepted by everyone. The possibility that the belief may be wrong, and that science may yet show it to be wrong, is not conclusive; for the legislature has the right to pass laws which, according to the common belief of the people, are adapted to prevent the spread of contagious diseases. In a free country, where the government is by the people, through their chosen representatives, practical legislation admits of no other standard of action, for what the people believe is for the common welfare must be accepted as tending to promote the common welfare, whether it does in fact or not. . . ."

A Minority Cannot Dominate the Majority

The defendant offered to prove that vaccination "quite often" caused serious and permanent injury to the health of the person vaccinated; that the operation "occasionally" resulted in death; that it was "impossible" to tell "in any particular case" what the results of vaccination would be, or whether it would injure the health or result in death; that "quite often" one's blood is in a certain condition of impurity when it is not prudent or safe to vaccinate him; that there is no practical test by which to determine "with any degree of certainty" whether one's blood is in such condition of impurity as to render vaccination necessarily unsafe or dangerous; that vaccine matter is "quite often" impure and dangerous to be used, but whether impure or not cannot be ascertained by any known practical test; that the defendant refused to submit to vaccination for the reason that he had, "when a child," been caused great and extreme suffering for a long period by a disease produced by vaccination; and that he had witnessed a similar result of vaccination, not only in the case of his son, but in the cases of others.

These offers, in effect, invited the court and jury to go over the whole ground gone over by the legislature when it enacted the statute in question. The legislature assumed that some children, by reason of their condition at the time, might not be fit subjects of vaccination; and it is suggested—and we will not say without reason—that such is the case with some adults. But the defendant did not offer to prove that, by reason of his then condition, he was in fact not a fit subject of vaccination at the time he was informed of the requirement of the regulation adopted by the board of health. . . . The matured opinions of medical men everywhere, and the experience of mankind, as all must know, negative the suggestion that it is not possible in any case to determine whether vaccination is safe. Was defendant exempted from the operation of the statute simply because of his dread of the same evil results experienced by him when a child, and which he had observed in the cases of his son and other children? Could he reasonably claim such an exemption because "quite often," or "occasionally," injury had resulted from vaccination, or because it was impossible, in the opinion of some, by any practical test, to determine with absolute certainty whether a particular person could be safely vaccinated?

It seems to the court that an affirmative answer to these questions would practically strip the legislative department of its function to care for the public health and the public safety when endangered by epidemics of disease. Such an answer would mean that compulsory vaccination could not, in any conceivable case, be legally enforced in a community, even at the command of the legislature, however widespread the epidemic of smallpox, and however deep and universal was the belief of the community and of its medical advisers that a system of general vaccination was vital to the safety of all.

We are not prepared to hold that a minority, residing or remaining in any city or town where smallpox is prevalent, and enjoying the general protection afforded by an organized local government, may thus defy the will of its constituted authorities, acting in good faith for all, under the legislative sanction of the state. If such be the privilege of a minority, then a like privilege would belong to each individual of the community, and the spectacle would be presented of the welfare and safety of an entire population being subordinated to the notions of a single individual who chooses to remain a part of that population. We are unwilling to hold it to be an element in the liberty secured by the Constitution of the United States that one person, or a minority of persons, residing in any community and enjoying the benefits of its local government, should have the power thus to dominate the majority when supported in their action by the authority of the state. While this court should guard with firmness every right appertaining to life, liberty, or property as secured to the individual by the supreme law of the land, it is of the last importance that it should not invade the domain of local authority except when it is plainly necessary to do so in order to enforce that law. The safety and the health of the people of Massachusetts are, in the first instance, for that commonwealth to guard and protect. They are matters that do not ordinarily concern the national government. So far as they can be reached by any government, they depend, primarily, upon such action as the state, in its wisdom, may take; and we do not perceive that this legislation has invaded any right secured by the Federal Constitution.

Laws Must Not Lead to Injustice or Absurdity

Before closing this opinion we deem it appropriate, in order to prevent misapprehension as to our views, to observe—perhaps to repeat a thought already sufficiently expressed, namely—that the police power of a state, whether exercised directly by the legislature, or by a local body acting under its authority, may be exerted in such circumstances, or by regulations so arbitrary and oppressively in particular cases, as to justify the interference of the courts to prevent wrong and oppression. . . . "All laws," this court has said, "should receive a sensible construction. General terms should be so limited in their application as not to lead to injustice, oppression, or an absurd consequence. It will always, therefore, be presumed that the legislature intended exceptions to its language which would avoid results of this character. The reason of the law in such cases should prevail over its letter" (*United States v. Kirby*). . . . We are not inclined to hold that the statute establishes the absolute rule that an adult must be vaccinated if it be apparent or can be shown with reasonable certainty that he is not at the time a fit subject of vaccination, or that vaccination, by reason of his then condition, would seriously impair his health, or probably cause his death. No such case is here presented. It is the cause of an adult who, for aught that appears, was himself in perfect health and a fit subject of vaccination, and yet, while remaining in the community, refused to obey the statute and the regulation adopted in execution of its provisions for the protection of the public health and the public safety, confessedly endangered by the presence of a dangerous disease.

We now decide only that the statute covers the present case, and that nothing clearly appears that would justify this court in holding it to be unconstitutional and inoperative in its application to the plaintiff in error.

"Society has no right to kill its geneti-
cally susceptible members, so Jacobson
ought to be overturned on moral
grounds."

The Court Failed to Give Due Consideration to the Risks of Vaccination

Stan Lippmann

Stan Lippmann was a student at the University of Washington
Law School at the time he wrote this viewpoint. He is now an
attorney who is still strongly opposed to compulsory vaccination
and has argued against it while running for various public of-
fices. Here, he presents his belief that vaccination is often harm-
ful, that the Supreme Court in the Jacobson *case relied on the*
prevailing opinion of medical authorities without considering
any other evidence, and that in declaring that it was impossible
to prove that vaccines are dangerous, it set a standard under
which no opponent could win. But, he says, the Jacobson *ruling*
did leave an opening for a new test case by stating that local
laws can be overturned if they are found to be unjust or absurd,
which in his opinion, is true of some that mandate vaccination
of adults.

A basic question of justice is whether any harm can know-
ingly come to an innocent group member for the good
of the group.... We were taught in our criminal law class of
the case of the *Regina v. Dudley & Stephens* in which the cast-
aways adrift in a lifeboat without food desire to and eat the

Stan Lippmann, "The Law of Vaccination—Toward Radical Reform," *VaccinationNews*
.com, January, 2002. Reproduced by permission.

cabin boy. The majority resorts to the murder and ingestion of its weakest member. When the party is rescued, the captain and mate are convicted of the murder. This case is included in the casebook to teach us that the very survival of the group is placed secondary in our system of justice to the principal of the sovereign rights of the individual to life. . . .

How is it that we are sacrificing the lives of many American citizens every day under the auspices of the National Vaccine Program? The death toll acknowledged by the Program during the past 7 years is 1,094, and this excludes the death claims which fail under the strict legal rules for establishing causality. Former Food and Drug Administration Commissioner David Kessler said in 1993 that only about 1 percent of serious vaccine reactions are reported. . . .

Although mandatory vaccination goes back into the nineteenth century and was upheld as constitutional by the U.S. Supreme Court in the 1905 *Jacobson* decision, it is under the motif of perpetual warfare: against Communism, Disease, Poverty, and Drugs; that whatever standards of medical ethics existed before have been thrown to the winds. . . The rationale for vaccination has always been that the alternative is worse: that more would die if the preventive measure of vaccination were not taken. Taken to its logical extreme, we today have the common opinion of medical doctors that to not have one's children vaccinated should be punished as a form of child abuse. Yet recalling the Open Boat example, it is criminal to sacrifice the one for the sake of the many, no matter what the cost/benefit ratio is claimed to be. This type of utilitarian analysis is fundamentally against the Western cultural conception of justice. . . .

In *Jacobson* and its progeny, the doctrine of high medical authority is used to preclude new countervailing medical evidence, and thus presents the root of the problem of obtaining private justice in the modern Vaccine Court, i.e. the legal establishment of causation of the vaccine as the source of the injury or death. . . .

Basis of the *Jacobson* Decision

The leading case in the area of vaccine law is *Jacobson v. Massachusetts* in which a local mandatory smallpox vaccination law was upheld under the police power applied to public health. It is noteworthy that the famous *Lochner v. New York* case was decided differently during the following term. In *Lochner*, the police power of the state to promote public health was denied when it attempted to set limits on hours worked in New York bakeries. The Court ruled this to be an impermissible interference with the right of contract between the bakers and the bakery owners. An essential difference between the cases is that in *Jacobson*, he was required by law to be acted upon, whereas in *Lochner* the bakers were forbidden by law from doing something. The Court is placing greater weight with freedom to act than in freedom to refrain from acting. This is a slim distinction, since freedom to refrain from acting really is a form of freedom to act in accord with one's wishes. A more realistic differentiation which renders the two decisions intelligible with reference to one another is that in both cases, the commercial interests prevailed, that the economic activity, whether baking or injecting, was furthered by the decision. Implicit in both of the Court's decisions is the belief that baking and being injected with smallpox are risks too small about which to be overly concerned. Indeed, a large portion of the *Jacobson* case concerns itself with just this question of costs v. benefits of vaccination, and as such it set many of the standards for what are permissible demonstrations of the costs and benefits.

In *Jacobson*, the Revised Laws of the Commonwealth provided that "the board of health of a city or town, if, in its opinion, it is necessary for the public health or safety, shall require and enforce the vaccination and revaccination of all the inhabitants thereof, and shall provide them with the means of free vaccination. Whoever, being over twenty-one years of age and not under guardianship, refuses or neglects to comply with such requirement shall forfeit $5." Jacobson is obviously arguing on principle, not over the size of the fine but his right to life and liberty. As it happened, he and his son had had the direct experience of having already been seriously injured by previous smallpox injections. An exception was made in favor of "children who present a certificate, signed by a registered physician, that they are unfit subjects for vaccination." From this limited exception we already see the illogic of setting fixed sets of rules. Why should an unfit 17-year-old automatically become a fit 18-year-old? In fact the risk of serious adverse events at least in some vaccines increases with age. . . .

Jacobson's Defense

Jacobson defended his refusal on three separate grounds. He claimed that the particular section of the statute of Massachusetts in question was in derogation of rights secured by the preamble of the Constitution of the United States; that one of the declared objects of the Constitution was to secure the blessings of liberty to all under the sovereign jurisdiction and authority of the United States, no power can be exerted to that end by the United States, unless, apart from the preamble, it be found in the body of the Constitution. Knowing from his own experience that he would place his own life in jeopardy by obeying, he knew he was in the Open Boat dilemma. But the Supreme Court declined to give credence to his assertion. The Court also passed without discussion the suggestion that the statute is opposed to the spirit of the Constitution. Was the spirit of the Constitution, as argued by the Federalist Papers, to protect the minority from the democratic majority? In historical realty protection of minority rights began as protecting the property owners, who are the minority. Since the modern civil rights movement, the idea of the protection of minorities has been reinterpreted to extend protected status to blacks, Hispanics, and women. It is yet to consider the special protection for genetic minorities, who are more real than racial minorities in a biologic sense. . . . The susceptibility to harm from the rubella virus seems to be related to the presence of certain genes in the individual. But in 1905, the Court, finding no violation of the Constitutional spirit apparent to it, quoted an earlier case in answer, "Undoubtedly, as observed by Chief Justice Marshall, speaking for the Court in *Sturges v. Crowninshield*, 'the spirit of an instrument, especially of a constitution, is to be respected not less than its letter; yet the spirit is to be collected chiefly from its words.' We have no need in this case to go beyond the plain, obvious meaning of the words in those provisions of the Constitution which, it is contended, must control our decision." Jacobson also defends his action under the due process clause of the 14th amendment. The Court does not answer this defense meaningfully either.

The Court then proceeds to consider Jacobson's offers of proof why he should not be compelled to take the smallpox vaccine. The Court found that the ninth of his propositions which he offered to prove, as to what vaccination consists of, was nothing more than a fact of common knowledge, upon which the statute is founded, and proof of it was unnecessary and immaterial. The Court here demonstrates how a little knowledge is a dangerous thing. It is still to this day not a clear what vaccine is made of. It is highly secretive business; in the case of the polio vaccine, it has turned out to have been contaminated with SV40 monkey virus. And it can be reasonably inferred that there are other as yet undiscovered organisms grown in the petri dish in the laboratory.

The Court then considers Jacobson's thirteenth and fourteenth offers of proof involved matters depending upon his personal opinion, which could not be taken as correct, or given effect, merely because he made it a ground of refusal to comply with the requirement. Moreover, his views could not affect the validity of the statute, nor entitle him to be excepted from its provisions. . . .

Next, the Court considered the other eleven propositions which all relate to alleged injurious or dangerous effects of vaccination. The defendant "offered to prove and show by competent evidence" these so called facts. But the Court declared that the only "competent evidence" that could be presented to the Court to prove these propositions was the testimony of experts giving their opinions. The Court declares that for nearly a century most of the members of the medical profession have regarded vaccination, repeated after intervals, as a preventive of smallpox; that, while they have recognized the possibility of injury to an individual from carelessness in the performance of it, or even in a conceivable case without carelessness, they generally have considered the risk of such an injury too small to be seriously weighed as against the benefits coming from the discreet and proper use of the preventive; and that not only the medical profession and the people generally have for a long time entertained these opinions, but legislatures and courts have acted upon them with general unanimity. If the defendant had been permitted to introduce such expert testimony as he had in support of these several propositions, it could not have changed the result.

An Impossible Standard of Proof

The Court seems to be saying a number of interesting things here. The Court declares a priori that it is impossible to prove that vaccines are dangerous. Why should not the individual confronted with authority be free from the possibility of harm? How is it that we allow human sacrifice? It seems incongruent with the radical individualism. But part of the resolution of this puzzle is in that we are forced to be gamblers to be winners. And we can say, it won't happen to me, the odds against are 1 in a million. And tough luck on that loser, I'm not going to get this disease. . . . Here again it's the doctrine of high medical authority, even necessarily overriding whatever experts had to say, weighed against what "everybody knows."

This standard is striking in that the standard proof necessary to prevail is impossible to achieve, and that everybody accepts it. But this everybody accepts it doctrine is weak. It disallows the discovery of new evidence of risk. And it accepts without question the idea that human sacrifice is an acceptable social regulation. But human sacrifice is ultimately an anti-social act. Over the past seven years, U.S. courts have now found vaccine responsible for more than a thousand dead and 7,000 wounded. . . .

The Court goes on to argue that the welfare of the many should be honored by restraining the non-complying social members. The problem here is that Jacobson was not doing anything to hurt anyone else, he was just existing in Cambridge. It is he who sought to restrain the authorities. The Court mentions that there are some times when a man is free [not] to submit to authority, but it just doesn't go deep to the essence of when such a condition obtains. Jacobson felt that his life was in immediate danger based on his own concrete experiences. If there is any time for the exercise of this form of resistance, this is it. It is interesting to see how the Court says what everybody knows, the state court must know and we must know. What it is that everyone must know is what high medical authority states. Again there is no consideration to the fundamental right to life.

The Court then goes through an exhaustive list of cost/benefit studies to justify its conclusion that the vaccine program must continue. But a republican form is opposed to the tyranny of the majority. It is the protection of the minority upon which the whole concept of federalism rests. In this case, it is a genetic minority, let's say. Should they be rubbed out of the gene pool? Then the Court claims that the many will really be hurt by the few who don't participate in the vaccine program.

This is totally false. An exemption could be made for those who claim previous adverse reactions. The herd immunity theory does not require all to be vaccinated. . . . Besides, if the program were voluntary, the people would make an educated choice as to whether they want the shot or to risk getting the disease naturally.

A New Case Could Modify the *Jacobson* Ruling

The one saving grace of the *Jacobson* decision which would allow a new case to be made to limit a . . . vaccine program is that it requires that the general terms of the local law should be so limited in their application as not to lead to injustice, oppression, or an absurd consequence. So ultimately, the *Jacobson* case, which is still controlling vaccine law after more than 90 years, may be ripe for a case which would limit the holding by establishing a boundary beyond which the Court would find unjust, oppressive or absurd. . . .

Jacobson grants the states police power to mandate vaccination. Unless vaccines could be marketed which do not kill or seriously maim certain individuals, the Open Boat case discussed in the prologue should govern: society has no right to kill its genetically susceptible members, so *Jacobson* ought to be overturned on moral grounds. But the endgame of the vaccine racket may be achieved within the framework of *Jacobson*. It should be possible to find a test case which the Supreme Court would find to be unjust and absurd. . . . By winning such a case, a milepost would be set on what is permissible and what is not. For example, using MMR [measles/mumps/rubella vaccine] on adults for no really valid reason when it has never been tested on adults in a controlled study and is known to be dangerous to a significant fraction of the adult public is absurd and unjust.

"Beyond its passive acceptance of state legislation in matters of public health . . . was the Court's first systematic statement of the constitutional limitations imposed on government."

Jacobson Set the Standards Under Which Public Health Laws Are Constitutionally Permissible

Lawrence O. Gostin

Lawrence O. Gostin is associate dean, law professor, and director of the Center for Law and the Public's Health at Georgetown University Law Center. He is the author of several books. In the following viewpoint, he explains the influence of the Jacobson *ruling on public health law. That ruling strongly supports the power of state health authorities, he says, but it also defines the constitutional limits on such power. Health laws are permissible only if they conform to four standards, which Gostin calls public health necessity, reasonable means, proportionality, and harm avoidance, all of which remain in the modern era although the process of legally judging them is now more elaborate than at the time of* Jacobson.

Massachusetts enacted a law at the turn of the century empowering municipal boards of health, if necessary for public health or safety, to require the vaccination of in-

Lawrence O. Gostin, *Public Health Law: Power, Duty, Restraint*, Berkeley: University of California Press, 2000, pp. 66–71. Copyright © 2000 by the Regents of the University of California. Reproduced by permission of the publisher and the author.

habitants. The Cambridge Board of Health, under authority of this statute, adopted the following regulation: "Whereas, smallpox has been prevalent ... in the city of Cambridge and still continues to increase; and whereas, it is necessary for the speedy extermination of the disease ...; be it ordered, that all inhabitants of the city be vaccinated." Henning Jacobson, who refused the vaccination, was convicted by the trial court and sentenced to pay a fine of five dollars. The Massachusetts Supreme Judicial Court upheld the conviction, and the case was decided by the U.S. Supreme Court in 1905. Jacobson's legal brief asserted that "a compulsory vaccination law is unreasonable, arbitrary and oppressive, and, therefore, hostile to the inherent right of every freeman to care for his own body and health in such a way as to him seems best." His was a classic claim in favor of a laissez-faire society and the natural rights of persons to bodily integrity and decisional privacy.

The Supreme Court preferred a more community-oriented philosophy where citizens have duties to one another and to the society as a whole. Justice Harlan, writing for the Court, states

> [T]he liberty secured by the Constitution of the United States ... does not import an absolute right in each person to be, at all times and in all circumstances, wholly freed from restraint. There are manifold restraints to which every person is necessarily subject for the common good. On any other basis organized society could not exist with safety to its members. Society based on the rule that each one is a law unto himself would soon be confronted with disorder and anarchy. Real liberty for all could not exist under the operation of a principle which recognizes the right of each individual person to use his own, whether in respect of his person or his property, regardless of the injury that may be done to others. ... In the constitution of Massachusetts adopted in 1780 it was laid down as a fundamental principle of the social compact that the whole people covenants with each citizen, and each citizen with the whole people, that all

shall be governed by certain laws for the "common good," and that government is instituted "for the common good, for the protection, safety, prosperity and happiness of the people, and not for the profit, honor or private interests of any one man, family or class of men."

Support of Police Power

Under a social compact theory, then, "a community has the right to protect itself against an epidemic of disease which threatens the safety of its members." The Court's opinion is filled with examples ranging from sanitary laws and animal control to quarantine, demonstrating the breadth of valid police powers. The legacy of *Jacobson* surely is its defense of social welfare philosophy and unstinting support of police power regulation.

Jacobson is a classic case about separation of powers and federalism, and these doctrines were used to support deference to the legislative branch and to the states. The Court's political theory about separation of powers led to an almost unquestioning acceptance of legislative findings of scientific fact. Quoting the New York Court of Appeals (which had recently upheld compulsory vaccination as a condition of school entry), Justice Harlan argued that

[T]he legislature has the right to pass laws which, according to the common belief of the people, are adapted to prevent the spread of contagious diseases. In a free country, where the government is by the people, through their chosen representatives, practical legislation admits of no other standard of action; for what the people believe is for the common welfare must be accepted as tending to promote the common welfare, whether it does in fact or not. Any other basis would conflict with the spirit of the Constitution, and would sanction measures opposed to a republican form of government.

Under a theory of democracy, Justice Harlan would grant considerable leeway to the elected branch of government to formulate public health policy. The Supreme Court, relying on principles of federalism, also asserted the primacy of state authority over federal in the realm of public health. "[I]t is of last importance," wrote Justice Harlan, that the judiciary "should not invade the domain of local authority except when it is plainly necessary. . . . The safety and the health of the people of Massachusetts are, in the first instance, for that Commonwealth to guard and protect. They are matters that do not ordinarily concern the National Government."

The *Jacobson* standard, assuredly, is deferential to public health authorities. The Supreme Court during the *Jacobson era* upheld numerous public health activities including the regulation of food, milk, and garbage disposal. Beyond its passive acceptance of state legislative discretion in matters of public health, however, was the Court's first systematic statement of the constitutional limitations imposed on government. The *Jacobson* Court established a floor of constitutional protection. Public health powers are constitutionally permissible only if they are exercised in conformity with four standards that I shall call public health necessity, reasonable means, proportionality, and harm avoidance. These standards, while permissive of public health intervention, nevertheless require a deliberative governmental process to safeguard autonomy.

Standard for Public Health Powers

Public Health Necessity. Public health powers are exercised under the theory that they are necessary to prevent an avoidable harm. Justice Harlan, in *Jacobson*, insisted that police powers must be based on the "necessity of the case" and could not be exercised in "an arbitrary, unreasonable manner" or go "beyond what was reasonably required for the safety of the public." Early meanings of the term "necessity" are consistent with the exercise of police powers: to necessitate was to "force" or "compel" a person to do that which he would prefer not to do, and the "necessaries" were those things without which life could not be maintained. Government, in order to justify the use of compulsion, therefore, must act only in the face of a demonstrable health threat.

The standard of public health necessity requires, at a minimum, that the subject of the compulsory intervention must actually pose a threat to the community. In the context of infectious diseases, for example, public health authorities could not impose personal control measures (e.g., mandatory physical examination, treatment, or isolation) unless the person was actually contagious or, at least, there was reasonable suspicion of contagion.

Reasonable Means. Under the public health necessity standard, government may act only in response to a demonstrable threat to the community. The methods used, moreover, must be designed to prevent or ameliorate that threat. The *Jacobson* Court adopted a means/ends test that required a reasonable relationship between the public health intervention and the achievement of a legitimate public health objective. Even though the objective of the legislature may be valid and beneficent, the methods adopted must have a "real or substantial relation" to protection of the public health, and cannot be "a plain, palpable invasion of rights."

Proportionality. The public health objective may be valid in the sense that a risk to the public exists, and the means may be reasonably likely to achieve that goal—yet a public health regulation is unconstitutional if the human burden imposed is wholly disproportionate to the expected benefit. "[T]he police power of a State," said Justice Harlan, "may be exerted in such circumstances or by regulations so arbitrary and oppressive in particular cases as to justify the interference of the courts to prevent wrong, . . . and oppression."

Public health authorities have a constitutional responsibility not to overreach in ways that unnecessarily invade personal spheres of autonomy. This suggests a requirement for a reasonable balance between the public good to be achieved and the degree of personal invasion. If the intervention is gratuitously onerous or unfair it may overstep constitutional boundaries.

Harm Avoidance. Those who pose a risk to the community can be required to submit to compulsory measures for the common good. The control measure itself, however, should not pose a health risk to its subject. Justice Harlan emphasized that Henning Jacobson was a "fit person" for smallpox vaccination, but asserted that requiring a person to be immunized who would be harmed is "cruel and inhuman in the last degree." If there had been evidence that the vaccination would seriously impair Jacobson's health, he may have prevailed in this historic case.

Jacobson-era cases reiterate the theme that public health actions must not harm subjects. For example, a quarantine of a district in San Francisco was held unconstitutional, in part, because it created conditions likely to spread bubonic plague. Similarly, courts required safe and habitable environments for persons subject to isolation on theory that public health powers are designed to promote well-being, and not to punish the individual. . . .

Jacobson, as explained earlier, established a floor of constitutional protection for individual rights, including four standards of judicial review: necessity, reasonable methods, proportionality, and harm avoidance. Arguably, these standards remain in the modern constitutional era, but the Supreme Court has developed a far more elaborate system of constitutional adjudication.

"Public health programs that are based on force are a relic of the 19th century; 21st-century public health depends on good science, good communication, and trust in public health officials to tell the truth."

The Basis for Balancing Between Public Health Needs and Constitutional Liberties Has Changed Since *Jacobson*

Wendy K. Mariner, George J. Annas, and Leonard H. Glantz

Wendy K. Mariner, George J. Annas, and Leonard H. Glantz are professors of health law at Boston University Law School. In the following viewpoint, they explain how the circumstances have changed in the hundred years since the Supreme Court ruled on the Jacobson *case, and whether similar cases would be decided in the same way today in the light of subsequent rulings. Some would, but many more factors would have to be considered than were significant in 1905. Moreover, they say that an important difference exists between health laws intended to prevent a person from harming other people and those intended to protect only the health of the individual; only the former are justifiable. In their opinion, preserving public health in the twenty-first century requires preserving respect for personal liberty.*

Wendy K. Mariner, George J. Annas, and Leonard H. Glantz, "*Jacobson v. Massachusetts:* It's Not Your Great-Great-Grandfather's Public Health Law," *American Journal of Public Health*, April 2005. Reprinted with permission from the American Public Health Association.

One hundred years ago, in *Jacobson v. Massachusetts*, the U.S. Supreme Court upheld the Cambridge, Massachusetts, Board of Health's authority to require vaccination against smallpox during a smallpox epidemic. *Jacobson* was one of the few Supreme Court cases before 1960 in which a citizen challenged the state's authority to impose mandatory restrictions on personal liberty for public health purposes. What might such a case teach us today? First, it raises timeless questions about the power of state government to take specific action to protect the public's health and the Constitution's protection of personal liberty. What limits state power? What does constitutionally protected liberty include? Second, answers to these questions can change as scientific knowledge, social institutions, and constitutional jurisprudence progress. A comparison of answers to these questions 100 years ago and today shows how public health and constitutional law have evolved to better protect both health and human rights.

An Earlier Time

Jacobson was decided in 1905, when infectious diseases were the leading cause of death and public health programs were organized primarily at the state and community levels. The federal government had comparatively little involvement in health matters, other than preventing ships from bringing diseases such as yellow fever into the nation's ports. Few weapons existed to combat epidemics. There was no Food and Drug Administration (FDA), no regulation of research, and no doctrine of informed consent. The Flexner Report was 5 years in the future, medicine would have little to offer until sulfonamides were developed in the 1930s, and most vaccines would not be available for almost half a century. Hospitals were only beginning to take their modern form, and people who had mental illnesses were often shut away in asylums. Contraception and interracial marriage were crimes, women did not have the right to vote, and Jim Crow laws prevented African American men from exercising constitutional rights that it took the Civil War to win.

Today, smallpox has been eradicated. The major causes of death are chronic diseases and trauma, which are influenced by multiple factors, including environment, occupation, socio-economic status, race/ethnicity, diet, behavior, and political inequality. Immunizations prevent many infectious diseases, and new outbreaks are most likely to result from global travel, laboratory accidents, or even criminal acts. Scientific advances have produced an array of health care facilities, drugs, vaccines, and technologies to prevent and treat health problems. Much of the responsibility for regulating the safety of the workplace, air, water, food, and drugs has shifted to the federal government. Women have the right to vote and to decide whether to have children. Patients have the right to refuse medical treatment, and everyone has the right to be free from arbitrary or discriminatory detention.

The states' sovereign power to make laws of all kinds has not changed during the past century. What has changed is the U.S. Supreme Court's recognition of the importance of individual liberty and how it limits that power. Additionally, states have changed how they use their power and what they regulate as new health problems and solutions emerge. . . .

Smallpox Was a Real Threat

As the 20th century began, epidemics of infectious diseases such as smallpox remained a recurrent threat. A Massachusetts statute granted city boards of health the authority to require vaccination "when necessary for public health or safety." In 1902, when smallpox surged in Cambridge, the city's board of health issued an order pursuant to this authority that required all adults to be vaccinated to halt the disease. The statutory penalty for refusing vaccination was a monetary fine of $5 (about $100 today). There was no provision for actually forcing vaccination on any person.

Henning Jacobson refused vaccination, claiming that he and his son had had bad reactions to earlier vaccinations. The

Massachusetts Supreme Judicial Court found it unnecessary to worry about any possible harm from vaccination, because no one could actually be forced to be vaccinated: "If a person should deem it important that vaccination should not be performed in his case, and the authorities should think otherwise, it is not in their power to vaccinate him by force, and the worst that could happen to him under the statute would be the payment of $5." Jacobson was fined, and he appealed to the U.S. Supreme Court.

The Supreme Court had no difficulty upholding the state's power to grant the board of health authority to order a general vaccination program during an epidemic. No one disputed, and the Constitution confirmed, that states retained all the sovereign authority they had not ceded to the national government in the Constitution. There had never been any doubt that, subject to constitutional limitations, states had authority to legislate with respect to all matters within their geographic boundaries, or to police their internal affairs, which Chief Justice Marshall referred to as the "police power." During the 1800s, the Supreme Court confirmed that this power included the power to pass laws that promote the "health, peace, morals, education and good order of the people." Most early Supreme Court cases that involved state police powers, however, were disputes over which level of government—state or federal—had jurisdiction to regulate or tax a commercial activity. *Jacobson* was the rare case in which a state's jurisdiction was not questioned—because no one claimed that the federal government should control a local smallpox epidemic. Instead, the question was whether the state had overstepped its own authority and whether the sphere of personal liberty protected by the Due Process Clause of the 14th Amendment included the right to refuse vaccination.

Justice Harlan stated the question before the Court: "Is this statute . . . inconsistent with the liberty which the Constitution of the United States secures to every person against deprivation by the State?" Harlan confirmed that the Constitution protects individual liberty and that liberty is not "an absolute right in each person to be, in all times and in all circumstances, wholly free from restraint":

> There is, of course, a sphere within which the individual may assert the supremacy of his own will and rightfully dispute the authority of any human government, especially of any free government existing under a written constitution. But it is equally true that in every well-ordered society charged with the duty of conserving the safety of its members the rights of the individual in respect of his liberty may at times, under the pressure of great dangers, be subjected to such restraint to be enforced by reasonable regulations, as the safety of the general public may demand.

Thus, the more specific questions were whether the safety of the public justified this particular restriction and whether it was enforceable by reasonable regulations. The Court answered *yes* to both questions. It noted that the vaccination law applied "only when, in the opinion of the Board of Health, that was necessary for the public health or the public safety." The board of health was qualified to make that judgment, and, consistent with its own precedents, the Court said that it was the legislature's prerogative to determine *how* to control the epidemic, as long as it did not act in an unreasonable, arbitrary or oppressive manner. Vaccination was a reasonable means of control: "The state legislature proceeded upon the theory which recognized vaccination as at least an effective if not the best known way in which to meet and suppress the evils of a smallpox epidemic that imperiled an entire population."

The Court nonetheless concluded with a note of caution:

> The police power of a State, whether exercised by the legislature, or by a local body acting under its authority, may be exerted in such circumstances or by regulations so arbitrary

and oppressive in particular cases as to justify the interference of the courts to prevent wrong and oppression.

For example, it noted that the law should not be understood to apply to anyone who could show that vaccination would impair his health or probably cause his death.

In most respects, *Jacobson* was an easy case. The decision held that a state may require healthy adults to accept an effective vaccination when an existing epidemic endangers a community's population. As with all court decisions, what this "means" is a matter of interpretation. *Jacobson* may be what [scholar C.R.] Sunstein called a narrow and shallow decision—narrow because it is not intended to apply to a broad range of legislation, and shallow because it does not explicitly rely on a general theory of constitutional interpretation to justify its result. People who have quite different world views or philosophies can accept the decision because it need not require the same result for different laws or in different circumstances. Not surprisingly, judges and scholars emphasize different language in the opinion to support different interpretations. . . .

Public Health Law Today

Given the changes in constitutional law, public health, and government regulation, what kinds of public health laws that address contagious diseases might be constitutionally permissible today? A law that authorizes mandatory vaccination during an epidemic of a lethal disease, with refusal punishable by a monetary penalty, like the one at issue in *Jacobson* would undoubtedly be found constitutional under the low constitutional test of "rationality review." However, the vaccine would have to be approved by the FDA as safe and effective, and the law would have to require exceptions for those who have contraindications to the vaccine. A law that authorizes mandatory vaccination to prevent dangerous contagious diseases in the absence of an epidemic, such as the school immunization requirement summarily upheld in 1922, also would probably be upheld as long as (1) the disease still exists in the population where it can spread and cause serious injury to those infected, and (2) a safe and effective vaccine could prevent transmission to others.

The legitimacy of compulsory vaccination programs depends on both scientific factors and constitutional limits. Scientific factors include the prevalence, incidence, and severity of the contagious disease; the mode of transmission; the safety and effectiveness of any vaccine in preventing transmission; and the nature of any available treatment. Constitutional limits include protection against unjustified bodily intrusions, such as forcible vaccination of individuals at risk for adverse reactions, and physical restraints and unreasonable penalties for refusal.

Ordinarily, there would be no justification for compulsory vaccination against a disease like smallpox that does not exist in nature. The Centers for Disease Control and Prevention's recent attempt to persuade health care workers to voluntarily accept smallpox vaccination failed, largely because of concerns about the risks of vaccination in the absence of a credible threat of disease. Protecting the country against a terrorist's introduction of smallpox would fall within federal jurisdiction over national security. The introduction of smallpox also could be a crime under both federal and state law. Assuming that an FDA-approved vaccine were available, there would be little, if any, practical need for a mandatory vaccination law. People at risk would undoubtedly demand vaccine protection, just as they clamored for ciprofloxacin after the (non-contagious) anthrax attacks in 2001. The real problem in such cases is likely to be providing enough vaccine in a timely manner. The same may be true for a natural pandemic caused by new strains of influenza, for example. On the other hand, if a vaccine were investigational, compulsory vaccination would not be constitutional, and people would be less likely to accept it voluntarily.

Likewise, a state statute that actually forced people to be vaccinated over their refusal, such as Florida's new "public health emergency" law, would probably be an unconstitutional violation of the right to refuse treatment. In the case of Nancy Cruzan, the Court assumed, without having to decide, that competent adults have a constitutionally protected right to refuse any medical treatment, including artificially delivered care such as nutrition and hydration. Even the state's legitimate interest in protecting life cannot outweigh a competent adult's decision to refuse medical treatment. . . .

Two Kinds of Laws

Such cases underscore an important difference between laws that are intended to prevent a person from harming other people, which can be a justified exercise of police power, and laws that are intended to protect only the health of the individual herself, which are unjustified violations of liberty. A committee appointed by the British government is reportedly considering a proposal to vaccinate children with vaccines that block the highs produced by cocaine, heroin, and nicotine. Which category might this proposal fit? Drug addiction is a public health problem but not a contagious disease. It is unlikely that the possibility of a person becoming addicted to drugs in the future would be sufficient to warrant compulsory vaccination, even if it is assumed that the vaccine would not affect ordinary intellectual or emotional function. The modern public health approach would be to provide education about drug abuse or to offer safe and effective medications in a voluntary treatment program.

Even in an emergency, when there is a rapidly spreading contagious disease and an effective vaccine, the state is not permitted to forcibly vaccinate or medicate anyone. The constitutional alternative is to segregate infected and exposed people separately to prevent them from transmitting the disease to others. Here again, modern constitutional law demands a high level of justification. The Supreme Court has long recognized that "involuntary confinement of an individual for any reason, is a deprivation of liberty which the State cannot accomplish without due process of law," and some justices have called freedom from such confinement fundamental in nature. . . .

As a practical matter, major new epidemics or terrorist attacks are likely to be considered national emergencies. In such circumstances, overreactions are likely and constitutional rights may be trampled, regardless of established law, which is what happened when the military forced Americans of Japanese descent into internment camps during World War II. . . .

In 2004, however, the Court was no longer willing to give government "a blank check." It found that even individuals who were being held as presumed terrorists were entitled to constitutional due process protections.

Lessons for Modern Public Health

One hundred years after *Jacobson*, neither public health nor constitutional law is the same. Programs essential to today's public health, such as those that regulate hazardous industries and products and that provide medical care, which would have been struck down in 1905, are routinely upheld today because they serve a legitimate public purpose and do not interfere with personal liberty. In contrast, deprivations of liberty that might have been upheld in 1905 would be struck down today. Public health now has better tools at its disposal: better science, engineering, drugs and vaccines, information, and communication mechanisms for educating the public.

The history of U.S. Supreme Court decisions about states' power to restrict personal liberty shows the different ways in which states' power can be characterized. At bottom, however, all doctrinal interpretations begin with 1 of 2 presumptions: (1) the state has complete power to do anything that is not expressly prohibited by the federal or its own state constitution, or (2) the state has only those powers granted to it by the people or that constitute an essential aspect of sovereignty for which governments are formed. Although traces of both views can be seen in the opinions of different justices, the Court has generally adopted the first view: the Constitution provides the only limit on state power. Thus, the Court's interpretation of what counts as a constitutional right assumes extraordinary importance. As Justice Charles Evans Hughes noted, "We are under a Constitution, but the Constitution is what judges say it is. . . ."

During the past decade, the Court has been reluctant to recognize constitutional protection for new aspects of liberty. Some scholars and conservative justices have argued that the Due Process Clause does not or should not protect personal liberty, such as the freedom to use contraception, and that states should have freer reign to impose restrictions on people. Others argued that, without such protection, we might as well not have a Constitution. Although the Court is not likely to soon abandon what it has already recognized, the renewed debate makes clear how fragile constitutional rights might be.

At a time when terrorism threatens the entire world, people may be easily convinced that their security depends upon giving up their liberty. People also may believe laws that restrict personal freedom will not apply to them. History supports the view that coercive laws have largely targeted disadvantaged minorities. Quarantine laws were most often directed at disfavored immigrant groups. During the 19th and early-20th century, people who were poor, non-white, or recent immigrants were widely believed to live in filth, intoxication, violence, and debauchery or were often blamed for harboring and spreading disease. Such attitudes may have surfaced when the Boston Board of Health sent police officers to inoculate "tramps" against smallpox. Police reportedly held some men down and beat others to accomplish their task. Although we may believe we are more enlightened today, similarly disfavored groups are targets of antiterrorism laws. . . .

The Bill of Rights was designed to protect individuals against abuses by the state, even when the abuses have the support of the majority. This is why constitutional protection of liberty remains so important. . . .

Public health programs that are based on force are a relic of the 19th century; 21st-century public health depends on good science, good communication, and trust in public health officials to tell the truth. In each of these spheres, constitutional rights are the ally rather than the enemy of public health. Preserving the public's health in the 21st century requires preserving respect for personal liberty.

"It is ... unreasonable to force individuals to be immunized with a vaccine of unknown safety, in order to protect against an attack that may never occur, against a disease that no longer naturally exists ... [so] such a policy does not withstand the rule set forth in Jacobson."

The *Jacobson* Ruling Would Not Permit Compulsory Smallpox Vaccination as a Defense Against Bioterrorism

Andrew B. Zoltan

Andrew B. Zoltan was a law student and an editor of the George Mason Law Review *at the time this viewpoint was written. In it, he points out that although in* Jacobson v. Massachusetts *the Supreme Court upheld the power of states to pass laws mandating vaccination, it also set forth limits to that power. It stated that among other conditions, such laws must be reasonably required for the protection of the public's health. The* Jacobson *case would be decided differently today, Zoltan says, because smallpox has been eradicated and so requiring vaccination against it is no longer reasonable. The only possible justification for vaccination would be as protection against bioterrorism. But experts disagree both about the likelihood of terrorists using smallpox and about the safety and effectiveness of the vaccine. Therefore, in his opinion, compelling smallpox vaccination would be ruled unreasonable under constitutional law.*

Andrew B. Zoltan, "*Jacobson* Revisited: Mandatory Polio Vaccination as an Unconstitutional Condition," *George Mason Law Review*, vol. 13, Spring 2005, pp. 744–752. Reproduced by permission.

Citizens have challenged mandatory vaccination laws on many occasions. Perhaps the most important such case is *Jacobson v. Massachusetts*, which held that mandatory vaccinations fall within the police powers of the states.

In 1902, a Massachusetts statute gave local boards of public health the power to require vaccination for the residents of their respective towns or cities. In response, on February 27, 1902 the Board of Health of Cambridge required all residents of the city to be vaccinated for smallpox. Henning Jacobson refused to be vaccinated, claiming that the statute abridged his privileges as a citizen, and deprived him of liberty without due process of law, thus violating his Fourteenth Amendment rights. The Supreme Judicial Court of Massachusetts overruled Jacobson's exceptions and sentenced him to pay a fine of five dollars.

On appeal, the Supreme Court of the United States upheld the verdict, holding that "[i]t is within the police power of a state to enact a compulsory vaccination law, and it is for the legislature, and not for the courts, to determine in the first instance whether vaccination is or is not the best mode for the prevention of smallpox and the protection of the public health." The Court defined police power as "a power which the State did not surrender when becoming a member of the Union under the Constitution." The Court found that when the Board of Health adopted the regulation, smallpox was prevalent in Cambridge and the disease was spreading. Because state police powers include regulations created to protect the public health, and the public health was threatened by smallpox, both the Massachusetts statute and the regulation of the Board of Health were valid, and the Board of Health acted within its state police powers to compel vaccination.

Jacobson offered the opinions of medical professionals who felt that vaccination had "little or no value . . . as a means of preventing the spread of smallpox." Stating that the value and efficacy of smallpox vaccine was a concern of the Massachusetts legislature, and not the judiciary, the Court did not consider Jacobson's opinions.

> The fact that the belief [that vaccines are an effective means to prevent and control the spread of smallpox] is not universal is not controlling, for there is scarcely any belief that is accepted by everyone. The possibility that the belief may be wrong, and that science may yet show it to be wrong, is not conclusive; for the legislature has the right to pass laws which, according to the common belief of the people, are adapted to prevent the spread of contagious diseases. In a free country, where the government is by the people, through their chosen representatives, practical legislation admits of no other standard of action; for what the people believe is for the common welfare must be accepted as tending to promote the common welfare, whether it does in fact or not. Any other basis would conflict with the spirit of the Constitution, and would sanction measures opposed to a republican form of government. While we do not decide and cannot decide that vaccination is a preventive of smallpox, we take judicial notice of the fact that this is the common belief of the people of the State, and with this fact as a foundation we hold that the statute in question is a health law, enacted in a reasonable and proper exercise of the police power.

Finally, the Court held that a minority of citizens cannot defy the decisions of their legislature, when the legislature acts "in good faith for all," if the minority's actions would endanger the welfare of the entire community. Holding that the safety and health of the people of Massachusetts are the responsibility of the state, and that they are not ordinarily concerns of the national government, the Court ruled that the Massachusetts statute did not violate the Federal Constitution.

Limits of State Police Powers to Compel Vaccination

Although the Court ruled that the mandatory vaccination statute fell within the state police powers of Massachusetts, the Court did proscribe limits to such power:

> [I]t might be that an acknowledged power of a local community to protect itself against an epidemic threatening the safety of all, might be exercised in particular circumstances and in reference to particular persons in such an arbitrary, unreasonable manner, or might go so far beyond what was reasonably required for the safety of the public, as to authorize or compel the courts to interfere for the protection of such persons.

Thus the Court set forth a reasonableness test for mandatory vaccination statutes. In *Jacobson*, the vaccination program was reasonable in light of the prevalence of smallpox in Cambridge, and the Board of Health had no motivation, other than to protect the public's health, when it enacted the mandatory vaccination program.

The Court also held that courts may strike down legislation designed to protect the general welfare only when it "has no real or substantial relation to [public health, morals, or safety] or is, beyond all question, a plain, palpable invasion of rights secured by the fundamental law." The Court found that the statute could not "be affirmed to be, beyond question, in palpable conflict with the Constitution." Finally, the Court repeated that state police powers have limits, and can be encroached upon by the judiciary, namely when the police powers are used in an "arbitrary and oppressive" manner.

Today the Outcome of *Jacobson* Would Be Different

Smallpox was eradicated seventy-five years after Jacobson was decided, making mandatory smallpox vaccinations no longer a reasonable measure to protect the public's health. In response,

CDC halted mass smallpox vaccination in the United States in 1971. However, the threat of terrorists using smallpox as a weapon may make the use of the vaccine a reasonable measure.

If Mr. Jacobson were told to roll up his sleeve and receive a smallpox vaccination in 2005, he would be able to refuse. In *Jacobson*, Justice Harlan wrote that a state's police powers "might be exercised . . . in such an arbitrary, unreasonable manner, or might go so far beyond what was reasonably required for the safety of the public, as to authorize or compel the courts to interfere for the protection of such persons." Now that smallpox is eradicated, there is no need to vaccinate against it in any country. The probability of contracting smallpox is zero, so there is no possibility of infection. Therefore, the burdens of adverse events associated with the vaccine outweigh the benefits of immunity to the disease conferred by the vaccine. There is no reasonable basis to compel someone to receive a potentially harmful immunization when the disease against which the immunization is directed no longer exists. Such use of a state's police power goes, as Justice Harlan wrote, "so far beyond what was reasonably required for the safety of the public, as to authorize or compel the courts to interfere." If Mr. Jacobson were to come before the Supreme Court today, he would not be forced to receive the vaccine, or to pay his five dollar fine.

Smallpox Vaccination and Bioterrorism

The only justification for mass smallpox vaccination today is for protection from bioterrorist attacks. . . . Biological agents have recently been used against the United States, when anthrax was mailed to residents of Florida, Nevada, and New York, and members of Congress. In December 2002, President George W. Bush announced a national smallpox vaccination program, which stated that "[a]lthough there is no reason to believe that smallpox presents an imminent threat, the attacks of September and October, 2001 have heightened concern that terrorists may have access to the [smallpox] virus and attempt to use it against the American public." The plan called for the voluntary vaccination of 500,000 health workers by mid-January 2003, and for voluntary vaccination of up to 10,000,000 health and emergency workers in the following ninety days. By July 18, 2003, only 37,971 civilians were vaccinated and the plan has been described as "stalled. . . ."

The possibility that smallpox could fall into the hands of terrorist organizations is obviously cause for concern. The proper approach to address this concern is a topic of debate.

Public health experts disagree about the likelihood of a smallpox attack and the need to vaccinate before such an attack occurs. Some feel that the risk and consequences of a smallpox attack, using a weaponized virus developed by the former Soviet Union, are sufficiently great so as to outweigh the potential costs and injuries associated with the smallpox vaccine. Others feel that [according to George Annas] the "potential for biological terrorism is real (i.e., greater than zero), but very low, and in almost any foreseeable attack the number of deaths is likely to be low (as evidenced in the only real biological attacks to date [i.e., the anthrax attacks], in which between zero and five people died)." Others [Stephen Smith] have used even stronger words: "The whole bioterrorism initiative and what it's doing to public health is a cancer, and it's hollowing out public health from within . . . This is a catastrophe for American public health." Some experts [Riccardo Wittek] have concluded that "[i]t is impossible to estimate how real this [smallpox] threat is."

The main difference between these views is the perceived probability of a smallpox attack, and the amount of damage such an attack would cause. This would present a troubling issue for a court to decide, namely whether it is reasonable for states to require smallpox vaccination. On one hand, the United States stopped routine smallpox vaccination even before the disease was eradicated, which shows that smallpox was not considered a public health threat even while it was still known to exist naturally. The use of the vaccine, and its associated risks, would, therefore, be inappropriate, since the disease no longer exists naturally and there is no evidence that any terrorist group truly does possess smallpox. On the other hand, a smallpox attack could cause fear and panic, and could lead to greater societal harm than that caused by the infection itself. By immunizing appropriate members of the population, a state government could prevent some of this panic. WHO Director-General Gro Harlem Brundtland stated that "[t]he risk of adverse events [from smallpox vaccination] is sufficiently high that mass vaccination is not warranted if there is no or little real risk of exposure." Therefore, WHO guidelines recommend against the vaccination of entire populations or large groups of emergency personnel. . . .

Forced smallpox vaccination would not likely be upheld because such vaccination is unreasonable. First, the likelihood of a smallpox attack is currently unknown because no one knows for sure if any terrorist group or enemy state actually has weaponized smallpox. Second, the impact of a smallpox attack is unclear because the disease is not transmitted from one person to another until the onset of rash and skin lesions. At this point the infected individual is obviously ill, and is in too much pain to remain sufficiently ambulant to spread the disease. Therefore, a smallpox attack may not lead to a rapid spread of the disease, and limits the possibility of "suicide bombers" purposely infecting themselves and spreading the disease by walking through crowded areas. Finally, the extreme age of the current vaccine supply precludes perfect information regarding the safety of the vaccine. Previously unseen adverse events associated with this old vaccine underscore this safety concern. It is, therefore, unreasonable to force individuals to be immunized with a vaccine of unknown safety, in order to protect against an attack that may never occur, against a disease that no longer naturally exists and can be effectively contained by quarantine and vaccination after an attack. Because forced smallpox vaccination is unreasonable, such a policy does not withstand the rule set forth in *Jacobson*.

CHAPTER 2

Affirming the Right of Competent Adults to Refuse Medical Treatment

Case Overview

Cruzan, by Her Parents and Co-Guardians v. Director, Missouri Department of Health (1990)

In 1983, Nancy Cruzan, a twenty-five-year-old Missouri woman, was seriously injured in an automobile accident. Although paramedics were able to restore her breathing and heartbeat, she suffered brain damage and never regained consciousness. After several weeks in a coma, she fell into what is called a persistent vegetative state (PVS), meaning that she had no cognitive function or awareness of any kind and there was no chance that she could recover. She was given food and water artificially, through a tube. After this had gone on for four years, her parents requested that the tube be removed so that she could die naturally. They knew she would not wish to be maintained permanently in such a state. Furthermore, she had previously told a roommate that if sick or injured she would not want to be kept alive unless she could live halfway normally.

The hospital staff refused to discontinue Nancy's treatment without a court order, so her parents went to court and received permission for the removal of the feeding tube. The state of Missouri, however, appealed this decision, and the Supreme Court of Missouri reversed it, ruling that because Nancy had not signed any papers saying what she would want, artificial feeding could not be terminated. Her parents then petitioned the U.S. Supreme Court for review of the case. By a 5–4 majority, the Supreme Court held that the state had the right to demand clear and convincing evidence that Nancy would prefer death to permanent unconsciousness and affirmed the Missouri court's judgment. (Later, more evidence was obtained, and she died following removal of the feeding tube in 1990.)

Although Nancy's parents lost the Supreme Court case, it is considered a landmark case that legally established the right to refuse medical care. It is generally called a "right to die" case, as it affirmed the right of competent patients—and incompetent (unconscious) patients whose wishes are documented—to stop life-sustaining treatment. But it did much more than that. Previously, although common law (unwritten law based on custom and precedent) and lower courts had generally held that people can refuse unwanted medical treatment, this had not been established as a constitutional right. In some states, a doctor could overrule a hospitalized patient's wishes if it appeared to be in that patient's best interests, although certain kinds of procedures did require informed consent. The usual practice was to provide maximum medical intervention. Because most of the Supreme Court justices in the *Cruzan* case declared that the right of competent patients to refuse treatment is protected by the Constitution, that changed. All states now have laws that allow people to sign advance directives specifying what treatment they do not want to receive if they become unable to communicate, and/or appointing a family member or friend to decide on their behalf.

In addition, the opinions of the Supreme Court justices clearly stated that the artificial provision of nutrition and fluids is a medical procedure like any other. This has proved to be the most controversial aspect of the case. Some people maintain that giving food and water is not the same as treatment, but legally, when it must be done by medical means there is no difference. Also, the Court made no distinction between PVS—which in itself does not cause death—and illnesses that are immediately fatal following the withdrawal of life-support equipment such as ventilators. These issues were hotly debated by courts, legislators, and the media during the 2005 case of Terri Schiavo, which the Supreme Court declined to review.

> "The principle that a competent person
> has a constitutionally protected liberty
> interest in refusing unwanted medical
> treatment may be inferred from our
> prior decisions."

The Court's Decision: Evidence of an Incompetent Patient's Wishes May Be Required for Termination of Life-Sustaining Treatment

William Rehnquist

William Rehnquist became a justice of the U.S. Supreme Court in 1972, and in 1986, he became chief justice, a position he held until his death in 2005. He was a strong conservative, was a supporter of states' rights, and was best known to the public for presiding over the impeachment trial of President Bill Clinton and for his role in Bush v. Gore, *the case that decided the 2000 presidential election. In the following viewpoint, he presents the majority opinion of the Court in the* Cruzan *case, which not only established in constitutional law the right of patients to refuse life-saving medical treatment but also ruled that a state may require clear and convincing evidence of an unconscious patient's wishes. Because there was no such evidence that Nancy Cruzan did not wish to be kept alive by artificial feeding, her guardians had no right to insist that it be discontinued, and the state of Missouri's refusal to let her die was therefore upheld.*

William Rehnquist, majority opinion, *Cruzan v. Director, Missouri Department of Health*, U.S. Supreme Court, June 25, 1990.

On the night of January 11, 1983, Nancy Cruzan lost control of her car as she traveled down Elm Road in Jasper County, Missouri. The vehicle overturned, and Cruzan was discovered lying face down in a ditch without detectable respiratory or cardiac function. Paramedics were able to restore her breathing and heartbeat at the accident site, and she was transported to a hospital in an unconscious state. An attending neurosurgeon diagnosed her as having sustained probable cerebral contusions compounded by significant anoxia (lack of oxygen). The Missouri trial court in this case found that permanent brain damage generally results after 6 minutes in an anoxic state; it was estimated that Cruzan was deprived of oxygen from 12 to 14 minutes. She remained in a coma for approximately three weeks, and then progressed to an unconscious state in which she was able to orally ingest some nutrition. In order to ease feeding and further the recovery, surgeons implanted a gastrostomy feeding and hydration tube in Cruzan with the consent of her then husband. Subsequent rehabilitative efforts proved unavailing. She now lies in a Missouri state hospital in what is commonly referred to as a persistent vegetative state: generally, a condition in which a person exhibits motor reflexes but evinces no indications of significant cognitive function. The State of Missouri is bearing the cost of her care.

After it had become apparent that Nancy Cruzan had virtually no chance of regaining her mental faculties, her parents asked hospital employees to terminate the artificial nutrition and hydration procedures. All agree that such a removal would cause her death. The employees refused to honor the request without court approval. The parents then sought and received authorization from the state trial court for termination. The court found that a person in Nancy's condition had a fundamental right under the State and Federal Constitutions to refuse or direct the withdrawal of "death prolonging procedures."

The court also found that Nancy's "expressed thoughts at age twenty-five in somewhat serious conversation with a housemate friend that, if sick or injured, she would not wish to continue her life unless she could live at least halfway normally suggests that, given her present condition, she would not wish to continue on with her nutrition and hydration."

The Supreme Court of Missouri reversed by a divided vote. The court recognized a right to refuse treatment embodied in the common law doctrine of informed consent, but expressed skepticism about the application of that doctrine in the circumstances of this case. The court also declined to read a broad right of privacy into the State Constitution which would "support the right of a person to refuse medical treatment in every circumstance," and expressed doubt as to whether such a right existed under the United States Constitution. . . . The court found that Cruzan's statements to her roommate regarding her desire to live or die under certain conditions were "unreliable for the purpose of determining her intent," "and thus insufficient to support the coguardians['] claim to exercise substituted judgment on Nancy's behalf." It rejected the argument that Cruzan's parents were entitled to order the termination of her medical treatment, concluding that "no person can assume that choice for an incompetent in the absence of the formalities required under Missouri's Living Will statutes or the clear and convincing, inherently reliable evidence absent here." The court also expressed its view that "[b]road policy questions bearing on life and death are more properly addressed by representative assemblies" than judicial bodies.

We granted certiorari ["review to make certain"] to consider the question of whether Cruzan has a right under the United States Constitution which would require the hospital to withdraw life-sustaining treatment from her under these circumstances.

The Right to Refuse Treatment

At common law, even the touching of one person by another without consent and without legal justification was a battery. Before the turn of the century, this Court observed that "[n]o right is held more sacred, or is more carefully guarded by the common law, than the right of every individual to the possession and control of his own person, free from all restraint or interference of others, unless by clear and unquestionable authority of law." *Union Pacific R. Co. v. Botsford.* This notion of bodily integrity has been embodied in the requirement that informed consent is generally required for medical treatment. Justice Cardozo, while on the Court of Appeals of New York, aptly described this doctrine: "Every human being of adult years and sound mind has a right to determine what shall be done with his own body, and a surgeon who performs an operation without his patient's consent commits an assault, for which he is liable in damages" (*Schloendorff v. Society of New York Hospital*). The informed consent doctrine has become firmly entrenched in American tort law.

The logical corollary of the doctrine of informed consent is that the patient generally possesses the right not to consent, that is, to refuse treatment. Until about 15 years ago and the seminal decision in *In re Quinlan*, the number of right-to-refuse-treatment decisions were relatively few. Most of the earlier cases involved patients who refused medical treatment forbidden by their religious beliefs, thus implicating First Amendment rights as well as common law rights of self-determination. More recently, however, with the advance of medical technology capable of sustaining life well past the point where natural forces would have brought certain death in earlier times, cases involving the right to refuse life-sustaining treatment have burgeoned.

In the *Quinlan* case, young Karen Quinlan suffered severe brain damage as the result of anoxia, and entered a persistent vegetative state. Karen's father sought judicial approval to dis-

connect his daughter's respirator. The New Jersey Supreme
Court granted the relief, holding that Karen had a right of
privacy grounded in the Federal Constitution to terminate
treatment. Recognizing that this right was not absolute, however, the court balanced it against asserted state interests. Noting that the State's interest "weakens and the individual's right
to privacy grows as the degree of bodily invasion increases
and the prognosis dims," the court concluded that the state
interests had to give way in that case. The court also concluded that the "only practical way" to prevent the loss of
Karen's privacy right due to her incompetence was to allow
her guardian and family to decide "whether she would exercise it in these circumstances."

After *Quinlan*, however, most courts have based a right to
refuse treatment either solely on the common law right to informed consent or on both the common law right and a constitutional privacy right. . . .

The common law doctrine of informed consent is viewed
as generally encompassing the right of a competent individual
to refuse medical treatment. Beyond that, these decisions demonstrate both similarity and diversity in their approach to decision of what all agree is a perplexing question with unusu-
ally strong moral and ethical overtones. State courts have
available to them for decision a number of sources—state
constitutions, statutes, and common law—which are not available to us. In this Court, the question is simply and starkly
whether the United States Constitution prohibits Missouri
from choosing the rule of decision which it did. This is the
first case in which we have been squarely presented with the
issue of whether the United States Constitution grants what is
in common parlance referred to as a "right to die." We follow
the judicious counsel of our decision in *Twin City Bank v.
Nebeker*, where we said that, in deciding "a question of such
magnitude and importance . . . it is [better] part of wisdom
not to attempt, by any general statement, to cover every possible phase of the subject."

The Fourteenth Amendment provides that no State shall "deprive any person of life, liberty, or property, without due process of law." The principle that a competent person has a constitutionally protected liberty interest in refusing unwanted medical treatment may be inferred from our prior decisions. In *Jacobson v. Massachusetts*, for instance, the Court balanced an individual's liberty interest in declining an unwanted small-pox vaccine against the State's interest in preventing disease. . . .

The Protection of Incompetent Patients

But determining that a person has a "liberty interest" under the Due Process Clause does not end the inquiry; "whether respondent's constitutional rights have been violated must be determined by balancing his liberty interests against the relevant state interests" (*Youngberg v. Romeo*).

Petitioners insist that, under the general holdings of our cases, the forced administration of life-sustaining medical treatment, and even of artificially delivered food and water essential to life, would implicate a competent person's liberty interest. Although we think the logic of the cases discussed above would embrace such a liberty interest, the dramatic consequences involved in refusal of such treatment would inform the inquiry as to whether the deprivation of that interest is constitutionally permissible. But for purposes of this case, we assume that the United States Constitution would grant a competent person a constitutionally protected right to refuse lifesaving hydration and nutrition.

Petitioners go on to assert that an incompetent person should possess the same right in this respect as is possessed by a competent person. . . .

The difficulty with petitioners' claim is that, in a sense, it begs the question: an incompetent person is not able to make an informed and voluntary choice to exercise a hypothetical right to refuse treatment or any other right. Such a "right" must be exercised for her, if at all, by some sort of surrogate.

Here, Missouri has in effect recognized that, under certain circumstances, a surrogate may act for the patient in electing to have hydration and nutrition withdrawn in such a way as to cause death, but it has established a procedural safeguard to assure that the action of the surrogate conforms as best it may to the wishes expressed by the patient while competent. Missouri requires that evidence of the incompetent's wishes as to the withdrawal of treatment be proved by clear and convincing evidence. The question, then, is whether the United States Constitution forbids the establishment of this procedural requirement by the State. We hold that it does not.

Whether or not Missouri's clear and convincing evidence requirement comports with the United States Constitution depends in part on what interests the State may properly seek to protect in this situation. Missouri relies on its interest in the protection and preservation of human life, and there can be no gainsaying this interest. As a general matter, the States—indeed, all civilized nations—demonstrate their commitment to life by treating homicide as serious crime. Moreover, the majority of States in this country have laws imposing criminal penalties on one who assists another to commit suicide. We do not think a State is required to remain neutral in the face of an informed and voluntary decision by a physically able adult to starve to death.

But in the context presented here, a State has more particular interests at stake. The choice between life and death is a deeply personal decision of obvious and overwhelming finality. We believe Missouri may legitimately seek to safeguard the personal element of this choice through the imposition of heightened evidentiary requirements. It cannot be disputed that the Due Process Clause protects an interest in life as well as an interest in refusing life-sustaining medical treatment. Not all incompetent patients will have loved ones available to serve as surrogate decisionmakers. And even where family members are present, "[t]here will, of course, be some unfortunate situations in which family members will not act to protect a patient" (*In re Jobes*). A State is entitled to guard against potential abuses in such situations. Similarly, a State is entitled to consider that a judicial proceeding to make a determination regarding an incompetent's wishes may very well not be an adversarial one, with the added guarantee of accurate factfinding that the adversary process brings with it. Finally, we think a State may properly decline to make judgments about the "quality" of life that a particular individual may enjoy, and simply assert an unqualified interest in the preservation of human life to be weighed against the constitutionally protected interests of the individual.

In our view, Missouri has permissibly sought to advance these interests through the adoption of a "clear and convincing" standard of proof to govern such proceedings. . . .

The State's Right to Require Proof of Patient's Wishes

We think it self-evident that the interests at stake in the instant proceedings are more substantial, both on an individual and societal level, than those involved in a run-of-the-mine civil dispute. But not only does the standard of proof reflect the importance of a particular adjudication, . . . the more stringent the burden of proof a party must bear, the more that party bears the risk of an erroneous decision. We believe that Missouri may permissibly place an increased risk of an erroneous decision on those seeking to terminate an incompetent individual's life-sustaining treatment. An erroneous decision not to terminate results in a maintenance of the status quo; the possibility of subsequent developments such as advancements in medical science, the discovery of new evidence regarding the patient's intent, changes in the law, or simply the unexpected death of the patient despite the administration of life-sustaining treatment, at least create the potential that a wrong decision will eventually be corrected or its impact mitigated. An erroneous decision to withdraw life-sustaining treatment, however, is not susceptible of correction. . . .

It is also worth noting that most, if not all, States simply forbid oral testimony entirely in determining the wishes of parties in transactions which, while important, simply do not have the consequences that a decision to terminate a person's life does. . . .

In sum, we conclude that a State may apply a clear and convincing evidence standard in proceedings where a guardian seeks to discontinue nutrition and hydration of a person diagnosed to be in a persistent vegetative state. We note that many courts which have adopted some sort of substituted judgment procedure in situations like this, whether they limit consideration of evidence to the prior expressed wishes of the incompetent individual, or whether they allow more general proof of what the individual's decision would have been, require a clear and convincing standard of proof for such evidence.

The Supreme Court of Missouri held that, in this case, the testimony adduced at trial did not amount to clear and convincing proof of the patient's desire to have hydration and nutrition withdrawn. In so doing, it reversed a decision of the Missouri trial court, which had found that the evidence "suggest[ed]" Nancy Cruzan would not have desired to continue such measures, but which had not adopted the standard of "clear and convincing evidence" enunciated by the Supreme Court. The testimony adduced at trial consisted primarily of Nancy Cruzan's statements, made to a housemate about a year before her accident, that she would not want to live should she face life as a "vegetable," and other observations to the same effect. The observations did not deal in terms with withdrawal of medical treatment or of hydration and nutrition. We cannot say that the Supreme Court of Missouri committed constitutional error in reaching the conclusion that it did.

Petitioners alternatively contend that Missouri must accept the "substituted judgment" of close family members even in the absence of substantial proof that their views reflect the views of the patient. They rely primarily upon our decisions in *Michael H. v. Gerald D.*, and *Parham v. J.R.* But we do not think these cases support their claim. In *Michael H.*, we upheld the constitutionality of California's favored treatment of traditional family relationships; such a holding may not be turned around into a constitutional requirement that a State must recognize the primacy of those relationships in a situation like this. And in *Parham*, where the patient was a minor, we also upheld the constitutionality of a state scheme in which parents made certain decisions for mentally ill minors. Here again, petitioners would seek to turn a decision which allowed a State to rely on family decisionmaking into a constitutional requirement that the State recognize such decisionmaking. But constitutional law does not work that way.

No doubt is engendered by anything in this record but that Nancy Cruzan's mother and father are loving and caring parents. If the State were required by the United States Constitution to repose a right of "substituted judgment" with anyone, the Cruzans would surely qualify. But we do not think the Due Process Clause requires the State to repose judgment on these matters with anyone but the patient herself. Close family members may have a strong feeling—a feeling not at all ignoble or unworthy, but not entirely disinterested, either—that they do not wish to witness the continuation of the life of a loved one which they regard as hopeless, meaningless, and even degrading. But there is no automatic assurance that the view of close family members will necessarily be the same as the patient's would have been had she been confronted with the prospect of her situation while competent. All of the reasons previously discussed for allowing Missouri to require clear and convincing evidence of the patient's wishes lead us to conclude that the State may choose to defer only to those wishes, rather than confide the decision to close family members.

> *"American law has always accorded the State the power to prevent, by force if necessary, suicide—including suicide by refusing to take appropriate measures necessary to preserve one's life."*

Concurring Opinion: Preventing Suicide by Force Has Always Been Legal

Antonin Scalia

Antonin Scalia became a justice of the U.S. Supreme Court in 1986, and as of 2008, he is its second most senior member. He is a strong conservative who believes in a strict interpretation of the Constitution, according to the meaning it had when originally adopted. In the following viewpoint, he concurs with the judgment of the Court in the Cruzan *case, which upheld the right of the state of Missouri to continue artificial feeding of Nancy Cruzan. He argues, however, that federal courts should not be dealing with the case because the Constitution says nothing applicable. It does not, he asserts, guarantee the right to refuse medical treatment even to competent patients, because traditionally the law has always allowed the government to prevent suicide. In Justice Scalia's opinion, there is no difference between suicide and allowing oneself to die for lack of treatment.*

The various opinions in this case portray quite clearly the difficult, indeed agonizing, questions that are presented by the constantly increasing power of science to keep the human

Antonin Scalia, concurring opinion, *Cruzan v. Director, Missouri Department of Health*, U.S. Supreme Court, June 25, 1990.

body alive for longer than any reasonable person would want to inhabit it. The States have begun to grapple with these problems through legislation. I am concerned, from the tenor of today's opinions, that we are poised to confuse that enterprise as successfully as we have confused the enterprise of legislating concerning abortion—requiring it to be conducted against a background of federal constitutional imperatives that are unknown because they are being newly crafted from Term to Term. That would be a great misfortune.

While I agree with the Court's analysis today, and therefore join in its opinion, I would have preferred that we announce, clearly and promptly, that the federal courts have no business in this field; that American law has always accorded the State the power to prevent, by force if necessary, suicide—including suicide by refusing to take appropriate measures necessary to preserve one's life; that the point at which life becomes "worthless," and the point at which the means necessary to preserve it become "extraordinary" or "inappropriate," are neither set forth in the Constitution nor known to the nine Justices of this Court any better than they are known to nine people picked at random from the Kansas City telephone directory; and hence, that even when it is demonstrated by clear and convincing evidence that a patient no longer wishes certain measures to be taken to preserve her life, it is up to the citizens of Missouri to decide, through their elected representatives, whether that wish will be honored. It is quite impossible (because the Constitution says nothing about the matter) that those citizens will decide upon a line less lawful than the one we would choose; and it is unlikely (because we know no more about "life-and-death" than they do) that they will decide upon a line less reasonable.

The text of the Due Process Clause does not protect individuals against deprivations of liberty simpliciter. It protects them against deprivations of liberty "without due process of law." To determine that such a deprivation would not occur if

Nancy Cruzan were forced to take nourishment against her will, it is unnecessary to reopen the historically recurrent debate over whether "due process" includes substantive restrictions. It is at least true that no "substantive due process" claim can be maintained unless the claimant demonstrates that the State has deprived him of a right historically and traditionally protected against State interference. That cannot possibly be established here.

At common law in England, a suicide—defined as one who "deliberately puts an end to his own existence, or commits any unlawful malicious act, the consequence of which is his own death," was criminally liable. Although the States abolished the penalties imposed by the common law (i.e., forfeiture and ignominious burial), they did so to spare the innocent family, and not to legitimize the act. Case law at the time of the Fourteenth Amendment generally held that assisting suicide was a criminal offense. . . .

Refusing Treatment Is the Same as Suicide

Petitioners rely on three distinctions to separate Nancy Cruzan's case from ordinary suicide: (1) that she is permanently incapacitated and in pain; (2) that she would bring on her death not by any affirmative act but by merely declining treatment that provides nourishment; and (3) that preventing her from effectuating her presumed wish to die requires violation of her bodily integrity. None of these suffices. Suicide was not excused even when committed "to avoid those ills which [persons] had not the fortitude to endure. . . ."

The second asserted distinction—suggested by the recent cases canvassed by the Court concerning the right to refuse treatment,—relies on the dichotomy between action and inaction. Suicide, it is said, consists of an affirmative act to end one's life; refusing treatment is not an affirmative act "causing" death, but merely a passive acceptance of the natural process of dying. I readily acknowledge that the distinction between action and inaction has some bearing upon the legislative judgment of what ought to be prevented as suicide—though even there it would seem to me unreasonable to draw the line precisely between action and inaction, rather than between various forms of inaction. It would not make much sense to say that one may not kill oneself by walking into the sea, but may sit on the beach until submerged by the incoming tide; or that one may not intentionally lock oneself into a cold storage locker, but may refrain from coming indoors when the temperature drops below freezing. Even as a legislative matter, in other words, the intelligent line does not fall between action and inaction, but between those forms of inaction that consist of abstaining from "ordinary" care and those that consist of abstaining from "excessive" or "heroic" measures. Unlike action vs. inaction, that is not a line to be discerned by logic or legal analysis, and we should not pretend that it is.

But to return to the principal point for present purposes: the irrelevance of the action-inaction distinction. Starving oneself to death is no different from putting a gun to one's temple as far as the common law definition of suicide is concerned; the cause of death in both cases is the suicide's conscious decision to "pu[t] an end to his own existence. . . ." A physician, moreover, could be criminally liable for failure to provide care that could have extended the patient's life, even if death was immediately caused by the underlying disease that the physician failed to treat.

It is not surprising, therefore, that the early cases considering the claimed right to refuse medical treatment dismissed as specious the nice distinction between "passively submitting to death and actively seeking it. The distinction may be merely verbal, as it would be if an adult sought death by starvation instead of a drug. If the State may interrupt one mode of self-destruction, it may with equal authority interfere with the other" (*John F. Kennedy Memorial Hosp. v. Heston*).

The third asserted basis of distinction—that frustrating Nancy Cruzan's wish to die in the present case requires interference with her bodily integrity—is likewise inadequate, because such interference is impermissible only if one begs the question whether her refusal to undergo the treatment on her own is suicide. It has always been lawful not only for the State, but even for private citizens, to interfere with bodily integrity to prevent a felony. . . .

It is not even reasonable, much less required by the Constitution, to maintain that, although the State has the right to prevent a person from slashing his wrists, it does not have the power to apply physical force to prevent him from doing so, nor the power, should he succeed, to apply, coercively if necessary, medical measures to stop the flow of blood. The state-run hospital, I am certain, is not liable under 42 U.S.C. 1983 for violation of constitutional rights, nor the private hospital liable under general tort law, if, in a State where suicide is unlawful, it pumps out the stomach of a person who has intentionally taken an overdose of barbiturates, despite that person's wishes to the contrary.

There Is No Constitutional Right to Die

The dissents of Justices Brennan and Stevens make a plausible case for our intervention here only by embracing—the latter explicitly and the former by implication—a political principle that the States are free to adopt, but that is demonstrably not imposed by the Constitution. "The State," says Justice Brennan, "has no legitimate general interest in someone's life, completely abstracted from the interest of the person living that life, that could outweigh the person's choice to *avoid medical treatment*." The italicized phrase sounds moderate enough, and is all that is needed to cover the present case—but the proposition cannot logically be so limited. One who accepts it must also accept, I think, that the State has no such legitimate interest that could outweigh "the person's choice to put an end to her life." Similarly, if one agrees with Justice Brennan that "the State's general interest in life must accede to Nancy Cruzan's particularized and intense interest in self-determination in her choice of medical treatment," he must also believe that the State must accede to her "particularized and intense interest in self-determination in her choice whether to continue living or to die." For insofar as balancing the relative interests of the State and the individual is concerned, there is nothing distinctive about accepting death through the refusal of "medical treatment," as opposed to accepting it through the refusal of food, or through the failure to shut off the engine and get out of the car after parking in one's garage after work. Suppose that Nancy Cruzan were in precisely the condition she is in today, except that she could be fed and digest food and water without artificial assistance. How is the State's "interest" in keeping her alive thereby increased, or her interest in deciding whether she wants to continue living reduced? It seems to me, in other words, that Justice Brennan's position ultimately rests upon the proposition that it is none of the State's business if a person wants to commit suicide. Justice Stevens is explicit on the point: "Choices about death touch the core of liberty. . . ." This is a view that some societies have held, and that our States are free to adopt if they wish. But it is not a view imposed by our constitutional traditions, in which the power of the State to prohibit suicide is unquestionable.

There Is No Constitutional Right Involved

What I have said above is not meant to suggest that I would think it desirable, if we were sure that Nancy Cruzan wanted to die, to keep her alive by the means at issue here. I assert only that the Constitution has nothing to say about the subject. To raise up a constitutional right here, we would have to create out of nothing (for it exists neither in text nor tradition) some constitutional principle whereby, although the State may insist that an individual come in out of the cold and eat food, it may not insist that he take medicine; and although it may pump his stomach empty of poison he has ingested, it may not fill his stomach with food he has failed to ingest. Are there, then, no reasonable and humane limits that ought not to be exceeded in requiring an individual to preserve his own life? There obviously are, but they are not set forth in the Due Process Clause. What assures us that those limits will not be exceeded is the same constitutional guarantee that is the source of most of our protection—what protects us, for example, from being assessed a tax of 100% of our income above the subsistence level, from being forbidden to drive cars, or from being required to send our children to school for 10 hours a day, none of which horribles is categorically prohibited by the Constitution. Our salvation is the Equal Protection Clause, which requires the democratic majority to accept for themselves and their loved ones what they impose on you and me. This Court need not, and has no authority to, inject itself into every field of human activity where irrationality and oppression may theoretically occur, and if it tries to do so, it will destroy itself.

> *"The right to be free from medical attention without consent, to determine what shall be done with one's own body, is deeply rooted in this Nation's traditions."*

Dissenting Opinion: The Right to Reject Medical Intervention Should Not Be Lost if a Person Becomes Incompetent

William Brennan

William Brennan was a justice of the U.S. Supreme Court from 1956 to 1990. He was an outspoken liberal especially noted for his support of civil rights and the expansion of First Amendment rights. In the following viewpoint, he dissents from the majority opinion in the Cruzan *case on the grounds that he believes the constitutional right to medical self-determination is fundamental and no other considerations can override it. He argues that artificial feeding is a medical treatment and that there are many reasons why a person in Nancy Cruzan's situation might not want to receive it. The only thing at issue, he says, is an accurate determination of her wishes, which he believes Missouri's procedural requirements do not provide. In Brennan's opinion, the state does not have the right to decide for her, and therefore the Court should not have upheld such a right.*

"Medical technology has effectively created a twilight zone of suspended animation where death commences while life, in some form, continues. Some patients,

William Brennan, dissenting opinion, *Cruzan v. Director, Missouri Department of Health*, U.S. Supreme Court, June 25, 1990.

however, want no part of a life sustained only by medical technology. Instead, they prefer a plan of medical treatment that allows nature to take its course and permits them to die with dignity"

[Rasmussen v. Fleming].

Nancy Cruzan has dwelt in that twilight zone for six years. She is oblivious to her surroundings and will remain so. Her body twitches only reflexively, without consciousness (ibid). The areas of her brain that once thought, felt, and experienced sensations have degenerated badly, and are continuing to do so. The cavities remaining are filling with cerebrospinal fluid. The "'cerebral cortical atrophy is irreversible, permanent, progressive and ongoing.'" "Nancy will never interact meaningfully with her environment again. She will remain in a persistent vegetative state until her death." Because she cannot swallow, her nutrition and hydration are delivered through a tube surgically implanted in her stomach.

A grown woman at the time of the accident, Nancy had previously expressed her wish to forgo continuing medical care under circumstances such as these. Her family and her friends are convinced that this is what she would want. A guardian ad litem appointed by the trial court is also convinced that this is what Nancy would want. Yet the Missouri Supreme Court, alone among state courts deciding such a question, has determined that an irreversibly vegetative patient will remain a passive prisoner of medical technology—for Nancy, perhaps for the next 30 years.

Today the Court, while tentatively accepting that there is some degree of constitutionally protected liberty interest in avoiding unwanted medical treatment, including life-sustaining medical treatment such as artificial nutrition and hydration, affirms the decision of the Missouri Supreme Court. Because I believe that Nancy Cruzan has a fundamental right to be free of unwanted artificial nutrition and hydration, which right is not outweighed by any interests of the State, and because I find that the improperly biased procedural obstacles imposed by the Missouri Supreme Court impermissibly burden that right, I respectfully dissent. Nancy Cruzan is entitled to choose to die with dignity. . . .

The question before this Court is a relatively narrow one: whether the Due Process Clause allows Missouri to require a now-incompetent patient in an irreversible persistent vegetative state to remain on life-support absent rigorously clear and convincing evidence that avoiding the treatment represents the patient's prior, express choice. If a fundamental right is at issue, Missouri's rule of decision must be scrutinized under the standards this Court has always applied in such circumstances. As we said in *Zablocki v. Redhail*, if a requirement imposed by a State "significantly interferes with the exercise of a fundamental right, it cannot be upheld unless it is supported by sufficiently important state interests and is closely tailored to effectuate only those interests. . . ."

A Fundamental Right

The starting point for our legal analysis must be whether a competent person has a constitutional right to avoid unwanted medical care. . . . Today, the Court concedes that our prior decisions "support the recognition of a general liberty interest in refusing medical treatment." The Court, however, avoids discussing either the measure of that liberty interest or its application by assuming, for purposes of this case only, that a competent person has a constitutionally protected liberty interest in being free of unwanted artificial nutrition and hydration. Justice O'Connor's opinion is less parsimonious. She openly affirms that "the Court has often deemed state incursions into the body repugnant to the interests protected by the Due Process Clause," that there is a liberty interest in avoiding unwanted medical treatment, and that it encompasses the right to be free of "artificially delivered food and water."

But if a competent person has a liberty interest to be free of unwanted medical treatment, as both the majority and Justice O'Connor concede, it must be fundamental. . . .

The right to be free from medical attention without consent, to determine what shall be done with one's own body, is deeply rooted in this Nation's traditions, as the majority acknowledges. This right has long been "firmly entrenched in American tort law" and is securely grounded in the earliest common law. . . . "Anglo-American law starts with the premise of thorough-going self determination. It follows that each man is considered to be master of his own body, and he may, if he be of sound mind, expressly prohibit the performance of lifesaving surgery or other medical treatment" (*Natanson v. Kline*) . . . Thus, freedom from unwanted medical attention is unquestionably among those principles "so rooted in the traditions and conscience of our people as to be ranked as fundamental" (*Snyder v. Massachusetts*).

That there may be serious consequences involved in refusal of the medical treatment at issue here does not vitiate the right under our common law tradition of medical self-determination. It is "a well-established rule of general law . . . that it is the patient, not the physician, who ultimately decides if treatment—any treatment—is to be given at all. . . . The rule has never been qualified in its application by either the nature or purpose of the treatment, or the gravity of the consequences of acceding to or foregoing it" (*Tune v. Walter Reed Army Medical Hospital*). . . .

Artificial Feeding Is Medical Treatment

No material distinction can be drawn between the treatment to which Nancy Cruzan continues to be subject—artificial nutrition and hydration—and any other medical treatment. The artificial delivery of nutrition and hydration is undoubtedly medical treatment. The technique to which Nancy Cruzan is subject—artificial feeding through a gastrostomy tube—involves a tube implanted surgically into her stomach through incisions in her abdominal wall. It may obstruct the intestinal tract, erode and pierce the stomach wall, or cause leakage of the stomach's contents into the abdominal cavity. . . .

Artificial delivery of food and water is regarded as medical treatment by the medical profession and the Federal Government. . . .

Nor does the fact that Nancy Cruzan is now incompetent deprive her of her fundamental rights. . . . As the majority recognizes, ante at 280, the question is not whether an incompetent has constitutional rights, but how such rights may be exercised. . . .

The right to be free from unwanted medical attention is a right to evaluate the potential benefit of treatment and its possible consequences according to one's own values and to make a personal decision whether to subject oneself to the intrusion. For a patient like Nancy Cruzan, the sole benefit of medical treatment is being kept metabolically alive. Neither artificial nutrition nor any other form of medical treatment available today can cure or in any way ameliorate her condition. Irreversibly vegetative patients are devoid of thought, emotion and sensation; they are permanently and completely unconscious. . . .

There are also affirmative reasons why someone like Nancy might choose to forgo artificial nutrition and hydration under these circumstances. Dying is personal. And it is profound. For many, the thought of an ignoble end, steeped in decay, is abhorrent. A quiet, proud death, bodily integrity intact, is a matter of extreme consequence. . . . For some, the idea of being remembered in their persistent vegetative states, rather than as they were before their illness or accident, may be very disturbing.

State Interest Does Not Outweigh Individuals' Rights

Although the right to be free of unwanted medical intervention, like other constitutionally protected interests, may not be absolute, no State interest could outweigh the rights of an individual in Nancy Cruzan's position. Whatever a State's possible interests in mandating life-support treatment under other circumstances, there is no good to be obtained here by Missouri's insistence that Nancy Cruzan remain on life-support systems if it is indeed her wish not to do so. Missouri does not claim, nor could it, that society as a whole will be benefited by Nancy's receiving medical treatment. No third party's situation will be improved and no harm to others will be averted.

The only state interest asserted here is a general interest in the preservation of life. But the State has no legitimate general interest in someone's life, completely abstracted from the interest of the person living that life, that could outweigh the person's choice to avoid medical treatment. . . . Thus, the State's general interest in life must accede to Nancy Cruzan's particularized and intense interest in self-determination in her choice of medical treatment. There is simply nothing legitimately within the State's purview to be gained by superseding her decision.

This is not to say that the State has no legitimate interests to assert here. As the majority recognizes, Missouri has a parens patriae ["father of the people"] interest in providing Nancy Cruzan, now incompetent, with as accurate as possible a determination of how she would exercise her rights under these circumstances. Second, if and when it is determined that Nancy Cruzan would want to continue treatment, the State may legitimately assert an interest in providing that treatment. But until Nancy's wishes have been determined, the only state interest that may be asserted is an interest in safe-guarding the accuracy of that determination.

Accuracy, therefore, must be our touchstone. Missouri may constitutionally impose only those procedural requirements that serve to enhance the accuracy of a determination of Nancy Cruzan's wishes or are at least consistent with an accurate determination. The Missouri "safeguard" that the Court upholds today does not meet that standard. The determination needed in this context is whether the incompetent person would choose to live in a persistent vegetative state on life-support or to avoid this medical treatment. Missouri's rule of decision imposes a markedly asymmetrical evidentiary burden. Only evidence of specific statements of treatment choice made by the patient when competent is admissible to support a finding that the patient, now in a persistent vegetative state, would wish to avoid further medical treatment. Moreover, this evidence must be clear and convincing. No proof is required to support a finding that the incompetent person would wish to continue treatment. . . .

To be sure, courts have long erected clear and convincing evidence standards to place the greater risk of erroneous decisions on those bringing disfavored claims. In such cases, however, the choice to discourage certain claims was a legitimate, constitutional policy choice. In contrast, Missouri has no such power to disfavor a choice by Nancy Cruzan to avoid medical treatment, because Missouri has no legitimate interest in providing Nancy with treatment until it is established that this represents her choice. . . .

The majority claims that the allocation of the risk of error is justified because it is more important not to terminate life-support for someone who would wish it continued than to honor the wishes of someone who would not. An erroneous decision to terminate life-support is irrevocable, says the majority, while an erroneous decision not to terminate "results in a maintenance of the status quo." But, from the point of view of the patient, an erroneous decision in either direction is irrevocable. An erroneous decision to terminate artificial nutrition and hydration, to be sure, will lead to failure of that last remnant of physiological life, the brain stem, and result in complete brain death. An erroneous decision not to terminate life-support, however, robs a patient of the very qualities protected by the right to avoid unwanted medical treatment. His own degraded existence is perpetuated; his family's suffering is protracted; the memory he leaves behind becomes more and more distorted. . . .

Missouri Court Ignored Evidence of Nancy's Wishes

Even more than its heightened evidentiary standard, the Missouri court's categorical exclusion of relevant evidence dispenses with any semblance of accurate factfinding. The court adverted to no evidence supporting its decision, but held that no clear and convincing, inherently reliable evidence had been presented to show that Nancy would want to avoid further treatment. In doing so, the court failed to consider statements Nancy had made to family members and a close friend. The court also failed to consider testimony from Nancy's mother and sister that they were certain that Nancy would want to discontinue artificial nutrition and hydration, even after the court found that Nancy's family was loving and without malignant motive. . . .

Too few people execute living wills or equivalently formal directives for such an evidentiary rule to ensure adequately that the wishes of incompetent persons will be honored. While it might be a wise social policy to encourage people to furnish such instructions, no general conclusion about a patient's choice can be drawn from the absence of formalities. The probability of becoming irreversibly vegetative is so low that many people may not feel an urgency to marshal formal evidence of their preferences. Some may not wish to dwell on their own physical deterioration and mortality. Even someone with a resolute determination to avoid life-support under circumstances such as Nancy's would still need to know that such things as living wills exist and how to execute one. Often legal help would be necessary, especially given the majority's apparent willingness to permit States to insist that a person's wishes are not truly known unless the particular medical treatment is specified. . . .

The Missouri court's disdain for Nancy's statements in serious conversations not long before her accident, for the opinions of Nancy's family and friends as to her values, beliefs and certain choice, and even for the opinion of an outside objective factfinder appointed by the State evinces a disdain for Nancy Cruzan's own right to choose. The rules by which an incompetent person's wishes are determined must represent every effort to determine those wishes. The rule that the Missouri court adopted and that this Court upholds, however, skews the result away from a determination that as accurately as possible reflects the individual's own preferences and beliefs. It is a rule that transforms human beings into passive subjects of medical technology. . . .

Finally, I cannot agree with the majority that where it is not possible to determine what choice an incompetent patient would make, a State's role as parens patriae permits the State automatically to make that choice itself. Under fair rules of evidence, it is improbable that a court could not determine what the patient's choice would be. Under the rule of decision adopted by Missouri and upheld today by this Court, such occasions might be numerous. But in neither case does it follow that it is constitutionally acceptable for the State invariably to assume the role of deciding for the patient. A State's legitimate interest in safeguarding a patient's choice cannot be furthered by simply appropriating it. . . .

A State's inability to discern an incompetent patient's choice still need not mean that a State is rendered powerless to protect that choice. But I would find that the Due Process Clause prohibits a State from doing more than that. A State may ensure that the person who makes the decision on the patient's behalf is the one whom the patient himself would have selected to make that choice for him. And a State may exclude from consideration anyone having improper motives. But a State generally must either repose the choice with the person whom the patient himself would most likely have chosen as proxy or leave the decision to the patient's family.

As many as 10,000 patients are being maintained in persistent vegetative states in the United States, and the number is expected to increase significantly in the near future. Medical technology, developed over the past 20 or so years, is often capable of resuscitating people after they have stopped breathing or their hearts have stopped beating. Some of those people are brought fully back to life. Two decades ago, those who were not and could not swallow and digest food, died. Intravenous solutions could not provide sufficient calories to maintain people for more than a short time. Today, various forms of artificial feeding have been developed that are able to keep people metabolically alive for years, even decades. . . .

The President's Commission, after years of research, concluded:

> "In few areas of health care are people's evaluations of their experiences so varied and uniquely personal as in their assessments of the nature and value of the processes associated with dying. For some, every moment of life is of inestimable value; for others, life without some desired level of mental or physical ability is worthless or burdensome. A moderate degree of suffering may be an important means of personal growth and religious experience to one person, but only frightening or despicable to another."

Yet Missouri and this Court have displaced Nancy's own assessment of the processes associated with dying. They have discarded evidence of her will, ignored her values, and deprived her of the right to a decision as closely approximating her own choice as humanly possible. They have done so disingenuously in her name, and openly in Missouri's own. That Missouri and this Court may truly be motivated only by concern for incompetent patients makes no matter. As one of our most prominent jurists warned us decades ago: "Experience should teach us to be most on our guard to protect liberty when the government's purposes are beneficent. . . . The greatest dangers to liberty lurk in insidious encroachment by men of zeal, well meaning but without understanding" (*Olmstead v. United States* [Brandeis, J., dissenting]).

*"At least five members of the Court ex-
plicitly recognized a constitutional right
to refuse life-sustaining treatment on
the part of competent individuals, and
. . . future Courts are likely to honor
this right."*

The Rights of the State
Should Not Have Prevailed
Over Those of the Patient

George J. Annas

*George J. Annas is a professor of health law and director of the
Law, Medicine and Ethics Program at Boston University Schools
of Medicine and Public Health. He coauthored an amicus curiae
(friend of the court) brief for Concern for Dying on behalf of the
Cruzan family. In the following viewpoint, he expresses his belief
that in its* Cruzan *decision, the Supreme Court violated the
rights of Nancy Cruzan and her family by supporting arbitrary
government restrictions that are inhumane. He argues that families and friends are best qualified to know what a patient would
want and to reject evidence offered by them is to deprive incompetent patients of any voice and effectively turn them into non-
persons. Annas strongly agrees with the dissenting opinion of
Justice Brennan, and in his opinion, the Court's ruling is a tragic
one with far-reaching consequences. The only positive aspect of
it, he says, is that a majority of the justices explicitly recognized
the constitutional right of competent patients to refuse life-
sustaining medical treatment.*

George J. Annas, "Nancy Cruzan in China," *Hastings Center Report*, vol. 20, September/
October 1990, pp. 39–41. Copyright © 1990 Hastings Center. Reproduced by permission.

Had the Cruzan family been in China when Nancy Cruzan suffered the accident that left her in a persistent vegetative state, and had China done to the Cruzans what Missouri has done to them, outrage would have rung throughout the United States. The commandeering of Nancy Cruzan's living body by the Chinese government would likely have been condemned by the White House, the State Department, and the Attorney General. Nancy's parents, who know and love her better than anyone on earth, would have been seen as her natural protectors, the state as an unpredictable predator. Most Americans would likely have found it easy to see that both her and Nancy's family's rights were being unconscionably violated, and have thanked God that we live in a free country where arbitrary governmental actions are restrained by a Constitution.

Yet the post-Reagan Supreme Court's majority seems to believe that while personal constitutional rights exist, the Constitution should not protect them against government restrictions that are related to a legitimate state interest and are not completely "irrational. . . ." The choice is between the rights of Nancy Cruzan and her family, and the interests of the state. How did the state prevail? Why are we moving more and more toward a government that sees citizens merely as means to its own ends?

Nancy Cruzan, like Karen Quinlan before her, is a young woman in a persistent vegetative state whose parents believe that she would not want to continue to live permanently unconscious. . . . The trial judge granted the Cruzans' petition to have tube feeding discontinued because he believed this is what Nancy wanted. The Supreme Court of Missouri, however, reversed on the grounds that the judge's decision was based only on the preponderance of the evidence (that is, it was more likely than not that Nancy wanted tube feeding discontinued), and not on a higher standard of proof, "clear and convincing" evidence, which the court said would have required Nancy herself to have expressed a specific decision about permanent comas and tube feeding before her accident. . . . The Cruzans appealed to the U.S. Supreme Court.

Before the Supreme Court

Chief Justice William Rehnquist wrote the five-to-four majority opinion of the Court, mischaracterizing the case as one involving the "right to die" and the right to "cause death." Without deciding the central fight to refuse treatment issue, he said, "for purposes of this case" the Court would "assume that the United States Constitution would grant a competent person a constitutionally protected fight to refuse lifesaving hydration and nutrition." This right was implicit in previous Court decisions, based on the liberty interest delineated in the Fourteenth Amendment. The core of the case, however, involved determining what restrictions the state could impose on the exercise of the right to refuse treatment by surrogate decisionmakers acting on behalf of previously competent patients. In the Court's words, the narrow question was "whether the U.S. Constitution forbids a state from requiring clear and convincing evidence of a person's expressed decision while competent to have hydration and nutrition withdrawn in such a way as to cause death." The Court gave four basic reasons in concluding that the Constitution did not prohibit this procedural requirement.

The first is that this evidentiary standard promotes the state's legitimate interest "in the protection and preservation of human life." The second reason is that "her choice between life and death is a deeply personal decision. . . ." The third is that abuses can occur for incompetent patients who do not have "loved ones available to serve as surrogate decisionmakers." And the fourth reason is that the state may properly "simply assert an unqualified interest in the preservation of human life. . . ."

The use of the "clear and convincing" standard of proof was upheld primarily by the argument that it is better to make an error on the side of continuing treatment. . . .

In conclusion, the Court held that even though "Nancy Cruzan's mother and father are loving and caring parents," the State may "choose to defer" only to Nancy's wishes, and ignore both their own views, and their views of what their daughter would want.

The Dissent

Justice William Brennan wrote a dissent for three of the four dissenting members of the Court shortly before announcing his retirement. Following traditional constitutional jurisprudence, Justice Brennan argued that if a fundamental right of a citizen is at stake, the state action limiting it "cannot be upheld unless it is supported by sufficiently important state interests and is closely tailored to effectuate only those interests." He chided the majority for not characterizing the "liberty interest to be free of unwanted medical treatment" as a "fundamental right," one that "is deeply rooted in this Nation's traditions." To restrict such a fight the state must allege more than a general interest in life because, as Justice Brennan argued, "the State has no legitimate general interest in someone's life, completely abstracted from the interest of the person living that life, that could outweigh the person's choice to avoid medical treatment."

Secondly, even if preservation of life is a legitimate state interest in this context, the Missouri scheme is irrational since it could lead to more deaths than current medical practice. This is because medical measures to sustain life, once begun, cannot be terminated without clear and convincing evidence of the patients' wishes, as long as they prolong life. Trials of therapy therefore are effectively discouraged by the Missouri scheme, a result that is irrational.

Justice Brennan argued that the only legitimate interest the state can assert in Nancy's case is an interest in determining her wishes. In his view, the Missouri scheme is designed not to determine her wishes, but to frustrate them. By permitting only her own statements as evidence, and by requiring "clear and convincing" evidence before they can be determinative, the state has effectively deprived her of all other evidence, including the best judgment of those who knew and loved her as to what decision she would make (substituted judgment), or what decision would be in her best interests.

Justice Brennan also believes the notion of erring on the side of life by "preserving the status quo" is untenable. As he noted, the "status quo" proposition itself begs the question: had artificial respiration and feeding not been applied in the first place, the status quo would have been death from the accident. Moreover, the Court implied that continued existence and treatment in a persistent vegetative state is either beneficial or neutral; whereas "an erroneous decision not to terminate life-support robs a patient of the very qualities protected by the right to avoid unwanted medical treatment. . . .[A] degraded existence is perpetuated; his family's suffering is protracted; the memory he leaves behind becomes more and more distorted."

Finally, Justice Brennan argued that the Missouri rules simply are out of touch with reality; people don't write elaborate documents about all of the possible ways they might die and the various interventions doctors might have available to prolong their lives. Friends and family members are most likely to know what the patient would want. By ignoring such evidence of one's wishes, the Missouri rule "transforms [incompetent] human beings into passive subjects of medical technology."

A Bloodless Opinion

Seventeen judges have now reviewed Nancy Cruzan's case. Nine favored the state, and eight favored her. I find Justice

Brennan's dissent both constitutionally correct and humanly compassionate. In its bloodless opinion the majority precludes the Constitution from acting as a "living document" that could protect its citizens from aggressive state power augmented by medical technology. Although states no longer have the legal authority to make slaves of people, they now do have a new authority to permit medical technology disconnected from any human purpose to make slaves of incompetent citizens. Medical technologies have taken on a life of their own and seem to have been ceded more rights to be used than previously competent patients have rights to have their families make decisions about such use on their behalf.

Nancy Cruzan can continue to be subjected to treatment she never consented to, and according to all who knew her would never consent to, for another thirty years or more to further Missouri's stated interest in protecting the lives of incompetent patients who, unlike Nancy, do not have "a loving family." Formerly, constitutional adjudication would have required that Missouri "narrowly tailor" rules that restrict fundamental constitutional rights. Rules designed to protect individuals without loving families, for example, could not have been used against individuals with loving families. Now all the state must show is that the rule is not irrational.

The grisliness of this tragic opinion is manifest by its impact on Nancy Cruzan and her parents. The Court knows that its decision will continue nonbeneficial and unconsented-to medical intervention, as well as continue the suffering of Nancy's parents. But it doesn't care. Deprived not only of her right to decide, Nancy Cruzan has also been deprived of the protective role of her family. By denying Nancy the right to have her family speak for her, Nancy herself is deprived of her only voice and is effectively made a nonperson. The burden of proof should be on the state to prove that the family is acting contrary to the patient's interests. It is cold comfort to conclude that no other state need follow Missouri's lead: the truth is, none of us is safe if the state of Missouri can inflict its will on Nancy and her family. The decision is also dishonest: in a country that still has forty million uninsured, and where steps are being taken every day to contain and cut medical costs and Medicare and Medicaid budgets, how can the notion that the state has an "unqualified interest in life" be seen as anything but hypocrisy?

The Missouri scheme now is an uncompromising . . . restriction requiring that medical care which prolongs life cannot be discontinued from any child or never-competent individual in the state. Moreover, if the state has an interest in sustaining Nancy Cruzan's life regardless of its quality, antibiotics, CPR, kidney dialysis, and even organ transplantation could be ordered over her parents' objections, should any of these interventions be needed to sustain her life. . . .

Is the News All Bad?

There are some positive aspects to the *Cruzan* opinion. At least five members of the Court explicitly recognized a constitutional right to refuse life-sustaining treatment on the part of competent individuals, and even with the retirement of Justice Brennan, future Courts are likely to honor this right. Five justices also see no constitutionally significant difference between various forms of treatment, and view the right to refuse life-sustaining medical treatment as encompassing tube feeding. This is good news, and states may no longer be able to require tube feeding under circumstances where they would permit other medical treatment to be withdrawn. . . .

Nonetheless, given that every indication is that Nancy Cruzan would have chosen either her mother or father to speak on her behalf, and given Justice O'Connor's belief that such a delegation would be constitutionally protected, it is an empty triumph of procedure over substance to deny Nancy Cruzan's parents the right to speak on their daughter's behalf. In fact the entire opinion can be read as placing form over substance. The lower court did not know that the standard of proof was clear and convincing evidence until the Missouri Supreme Court so ruled in the appeal, and would almost certainly have found that the evidence presented met the clear and convincing standard of proof. Justice O'Connor thinks it appropriate to leave the task of crafting procedures to "safeguard incompetents' liberty interests" to the "'laboratory' of the States." The problem, of course, is that Missouri has already created a Frankenstein's monster in its laboratory, and the Court has now said that the U.S. Constitution is powerless to prevent the monster from wreaking havoc.

"The publicity and concern generated by the Cruzan *case brought public focus to the inadequacy of protection for the right to refuse treatment."*

The Supreme Court Set a Legal Precedent for the Right to Refuse Medical Treatment

S. Elizabeth Wilborn Malloy

S. Elizabeth Wilborn Malloy is a professor of health law at the University of Cincinnati College of Law. In this viewpoint, she explains that in the Cruzan *decision, the right of competent patients to refuse medical treatment was recognized as a constitutional issue for the first time. Although the Supreme Court majority held that this right is not absolute, all the justices agreed that it involves the guarantee of liberty provided by the Fourteenth Amendment; they differed only on how it should be balanced against the interest of the government in preserving life. Thus, says Malloy,* Cruzan *strongly supports the proposition that state and federal courts should protect the right to refuse treatment. Because of the public attention surrounding the case, all the states passed laws recognizing that such a right exists.*

The doctrine of informed consent, which includes the patient's choice to refuse life-sustaining medical treatment, is well accepted today in certain contexts. The jurisprudence that has developed is a mixture of common law, statutes, and federal and state constitutional glosses. From these

S. Elizabeth Wilborn Malloy, "Beyond Misguided Paternalism: Resuscitating the Right to Refuse Medical Treatment," *Wake Forest Law Review*, Winter 1998. Reproduced by permission.

sources of law, culminating with *Cruzan v. Director, Missouri Department of Health*, the first "right to die" case to come before the United States Supreme Court, the existence of a fundamental legal right to make choices about one's medical treatment is now firmly established.

In the 1990 decision, *Cruzan v. Director, Missouri Department of Health*, the United States Supreme Court, for the first time, found a constitutional dimension to the right to refuse medical treatment and held that the constitutional right to liberty is implicated by providing medical treatment without the patient's consent.

In 1983, Nancy Cruzan suffered severe and irreversible brain damage in a car accident. Although doctors aggressively treated Ms. Cruzan, she was ultimately diagnosed as being in a persistent vegetative state—"a condition in which a person exhibits motor reflexes but evinces no indications of significant cognitive function." After six years without any sign of recovery, Ms. Cruzan's parents asked the state hospital to discontinue life support and allow her to die. The hospital refused the request without a judicial order supporting such an action. Although Ms. Cruzan's parents obtained a court order from the state probate court permitting the discontinuation of life-sustaining treatment, the Missouri Supreme Court overturned the order. The state supreme court determined that life-sustaining treatment could be removed only on clear and convincing evidence of the patient's desire to have the particular treatment in question removed under the circumstances faced by the patient. The Cruzans petitioned the United States Supreme Court for review.

Recognition of Right to Refuse Treatment

Writing for the majority, Chief Justice Rehnquist held that the Missouri requirement of "clear and convincing evidence" that the patient would want life-sustaining treatment discontinued before permitting termination of such care did not violate the

Due Process Clause of the United States Constitution. First, the Court recognized that one of the primary means of protecting the notion of bodily integrity is the informed consent doctrine. As a result, the majority decided that the "logical corollary of the doctrine of informed consent is that the patient generally possesses the right not to consent, that is, to refuse treatment." The *Cruzan* Court observed that "most courts have based a right to refuse treatment either solely on the common law right to informed consent or on both the common law right and a constitutional privacy right." Here, the Court dismissed the notion that the constitutional right of privacy includes a right to refuse treatment, and instead stated that the issue is more properly analyzed in terms of Fourteenth Amendment liberty interest. All nine Justices agreed on the existence of this liberty interest, disagreeing only on how it should be balanced with the state's expressed interests in the protection and preservation of human life.

The majority balanced Ms. Cruzan's right to refuse medical treatment against the state's interest in the protection and preservation of human life. The Court determined that Missouri had permissibly sought to advance its interests by adopting "a clear and convincing evidence standard in proceedings where a guardian seeks to discontinue nutrition and hydration of a person diagnosed to be in a persistent vegetative state." It reasoned that imposition of this procedural requirement was justified both by the importance of the rights involved and by the appropriateness of placing the risk of error on those attempting to terminate treatment, as an erroneous decision to withdraw treatment is more permanent than an erroneous decision not to withdraw treatment.

State Interests vs. Patient's Interests

The notion that the state has an interest in the preservation of human life independent of the patient's own interests led Justice Brennan and Justice Stevens to write spirited dissents. Justice Brennan, joined by Justices Marshall and Blackmun, rejected the clear and convincing evidence standard as unduly burdensome on patients and their families. In dissent, Justice Brennan asserted that the majority had undervalued the liberty interest at stake and had given too much deference to the state interest, permitting the state to develop procedural law inconsistent with the effective exercise of the right to forgo life-sustaining treatment. "[T]he State has no legitimate general interest in someone's life, completely abstracted from the interest of the person living that life, that could outweigh the person's choice to avoid medical treatment."

Justice Brennan contended that a state could not interfere with an individual's fundamental right to forgo unwanted medical treatment unless the state employed means narrowly tailored to a sufficiently important state interest. Although he recognized that Missouri had a legitimate state interest in Ms. Cruzan's welfare, Justice Brennan refused to recognize that this included a generalized interest in the protection of life. Likewise, Justice Stevens observed:

> However commendable may be the State's interest in human life, it cannot pursue that interest by appropriating Nancy Cruzan's life as a symbol for its own purposes. Lives do not exist in abstraction from persons, and to pretend otherwise is not to honor but to desecrate the State's responsibility for protecting life.

Although the Court recognized that the right to refuse treatment was not absolute, the *Cruzan* majority emphasized the important autonomy interest at stake in personal decisions concerning medical care and required the government to have some justification for burdening that decision-making.

Cruzan strongly supports the proposition that the state and federal courts should robustly protect the right to refuse medical treatment, even if they are not constitutionally obliged to do so. In fact, during the post-*Cruzan* era, virtually all courts have affirmed the right of competent and incompetent patients to terminate medical treatment.

The Legislative Response

The publicity and concern generated by the *Cruzan* case brought public focus to the inadequacy of protection for the right to refuse treatment. In response, Congress and state legislatures passed a variety of laws. In 1990, the same year *Cruzan* was decided, Congress enacted the Patient Self Determination Act ("PSDA"), a federal law requiring every hospital and nursing home to provide information about advance directives to all patients upon admission. The PSDA further required institutions to develop policies addressing advance directives and to notify patients of the substance of these policies.

State legislatures also began passing laws to help safeguard the right to refuse medical treatment. Today, all states and the District of Columbia have recognized the right to refuse treatment through the enactment of a variety of natural death statutes, including living will laws, durable power of attorney for health care laws, do not resuscitate ("DNR") order laws, and health care surrogate laws. In addition, medical organizations, such as the Joint Commission on Accreditation of Health Care Organizations ("JCAHO") now require that health care facilities create a mechanism to assist patients in the development of advance directives. The JCAHO designed directives such as living wills to give physicians information about an individual's treatment preferences. All of the statutes and regulations demonstrate acceptance by a majority of the public of the right to refuse treatment.

One primary failing of these statutes is that most people, for understandable reasons, fail to complete formal advance directives. A recent study estimates that between ten and twenty-five percent of the adult population in the United States has completed formal advance directives (with some estimates as low as five percent). Additionally, as noted earlier, even if a patient is one of the few who has completed an advance directive, no guarantee exists that the doctor will obey the directive. Indeed, some commentators have noted that a financial incentive may keep certain people—those with health insurance—alive despite their wishes. Finally, many of these statutes actually provide immunity to the physician who fails to obey an individual's living will or advance directive. Thus, although these statutes buttress the ideal of patient autonomy, they do not adequately protect the patient's right to refuse treatment, and they fail to provide an incentive for the medical profession to respect a patient's considered exercise of the right to refuse treatment. Thus, the statutes fail to address the real problem—physician ability to ignore a patient's wishes.

CHAPTER 3

Establishing the Right of Mentally Ill Defendants to Refuse Medication

Case Overview

Charles Thomas Sell v. United States (2003)

Dr. Charles Sell, once a practicing dentist, had been mentally ill for many years at the time he was arrested on counts of Medicaid fraud and, in a later indictment, conspiracy to commit attempted murder. In the past, he had told doctors that the gold he used for fillings had been contaminated by Communists, reported to the police that a leopard was outside his office boarding a bus, and complained that public officials were trying to kill him. He had been hospitalized and released several times.

At a hearing concerned with allegations that he had tried to intimidate a witness, Sell's behavior was extremely disruptive. His bail was therefore revoked, and he was sent to a medical center for federal prisoners, where he was examined and found to be incompetent to stand trial. When he refused to take antipsychotic medication, a psychiatrist authorized its forcible administration on the grounds that Sell's delusions could make him dangerous, that it was a necessary medical treatment, and that it would render him competent for trial. Sell filed a court motion contesting this. At the subsequent hearing, it was stated that he had recently made inappropriate remarks to a nurse that caused him to be considered a safety risk. An order permitting involuntary medication was issued, but it was stayed to allow him to appeal to the federal District Court. That court ruled that Sell was not dangerous, yet nevertheless upheld the order for him to be medicated against his will. This decision was affirmed by the Court of Appeals and later reviewed by the U.S. Supreme Court.

What the Supreme Court had to decide was whether forcing a mentally ill criminal defendant to take psychiatric drugs is a violation of his or her constitutional right to refuse medical treatment. It concluded that it is, except when certain conditions are met. And, said the Court majority, those conditions did not exist in Sell's case. Prisoners can be forcibly medicated if they are found to be dangerous, but only under limited circumstances can it be done just because the government wants to bring them to trial. Also, the adverse side effects of psychiatric drugs might impair a defendant's behavior during a trial and thus affect the trial's fairness. Finally, it was noted that Sell had already been confined for a long time (in fact, due to the lengthy appeal process, he had been imprisoned without trial for longer than the maximum sentence for the crimes of which he was accused). Therefore, in a 6–3 decision, the Court ruled that the order for involuntary medication could not stand.

This ruling has required major changes in the handling of mentally ill defendants—there now must be hearings to determine whether the standards are met under which involuntary medication can be justified. On principle, it has been hailed as a victory by many advocates of mind freedom. "By ruling in Dr. Sell's favor, the Court has vindicated the fundamental right of every American to control his or her own thought processes," said Richard Glen Boire, director of the Center for Cognitive Liberty & Ethics, a nonprofit law and policy center that had filed an amicus curiae (friend of the court) brief on Sell's behalf.

Others, however, have deplored the Court's failure to ban all involuntary drugging of the mentally ill solely for trial purposes. Judy Appel, deputy director of legal affairs for the Drug Policy Alliance—who had also filed a brief in Sell's favor—said the decision was a mixed bag that "gives prosecutors the tools to ask for, and trial courts to impose, a major violation of individual liberty."

"*[The constitution] will permit involuntary administration of drugs solely for trial competence purposes in certain instances. But those instances may be rare.*"

The Court's Decision: Mentally Ill Defendants Cannot Be Medicated Against Their Will Solely to Enable Them to Stand Trial

Stephen Breyer

Stephen Breyer became a justice of the Supreme Court in 1994. He is one of the more liberal members and is known for an approach to constitutional law focused on its practical consequences. The following viewpoint is the majority opinion of the Court in the case of Sell v. United States, *in which it ruled that although under some circumstances the Constitution permits the government to forcibly administer antipsychotic medication to criminal defendants solely to enable them to stand trial, those circumstances are rare and did not exist in Sell's case. Important government interests must be at stake, Breyer explains, and involuntary medication of the defendant must significantly further those interests. It must be unlikely that less intrusive methods would do so. Furthermore, the drugs must be in the defendant's best medical interest in the light of his or her condition. The government must show a need for treatment sufficiently important to overcome the individual's constitutionally protected interest in*

Stephen Breyer, majority opinion, *Charles Thomas Sell v. United States*, U.S. Supreme Court, June 16, 2003.

refusing it. Because this had not been done, the lower court's order for forced medication of Sell was not valid.

The question presented is whether the Constitution permits the Government to administer antipsychotic drugs involuntarily to a mentally ill criminal defendant—in order to render that defendant competent to stand trial for serious, but nonviolent, crimes. We conclude that the Constitution allows the Government to administer those drugs, even against the defendant's will, in limited circumstances, *i.e.*, upon satisfaction of conditions that we shall describe. Because the Court of Appeals did not find that the requisite circumstances existed in this case, we vacate its judgment.

Petitioner Charles Sell, once a practicing dentist, has a long and unfortunate history of mental illness. . . .

In May 1997, the Government charged Sell with submitting fictitious insurance claims for payment. A Federal Magistrate Judge (Magistrate), after ordering a psychiatric examination, found Sell "currently competent," but noted that Sell might experience "a psychotic episode" in the future. The judge released Sell on bail. A grand jury later produced a superseding indictment charging Sell and his wife with 56 counts of mail fraud, 6 counts of Medicaid fraud, and 1 count of money laundering.

In early 1998, the Government claimed that Sell had sought to intimidate a witness. The Magistrate held a bail revocation hearing. Sell's behavior at his initial appearance was, in the judge's words, "'totally out of control,'" involving "screaming and shouting," the use of "personal insults" and "racial epithets," and spitting "in the judge's face." A psychiatrist reported that Sell could not sleep because he expected the FBI to "'come busting through the door,'" and concluded that Sell's condition had worsened. After considering that report and other testimony, the Magistrate revoked Sell's bail.

In April 1998, the grand jury issued a new indictment charging Sell with attempting to murder the FBI agent who had arrested him and a former employee who planned to testify against him in the fraud case. The attempted murder and fraud cases were joined for trial.

In early 1999, Sell asked the Magistrate to reconsider his competence to stand trial. The Magistrate sent Sell to the United States Medical Center for Federal Prisoners at Springfield, Missouri, for examination. Subsequently the Magistrate found that Sell was "mentally incompetent to stand trial." He ordered Sell to "be hospitalized for treatment" at the Medical Center for up to four months, "to determine whether there was a substantial probability that [Sell] would attain the capacity to allow his trial to proceed."

Two months later, Medical Center staff recommended that Sell take antipsychotic medication. Sell refused to do so. The staff sought permission to administer the medication against Sell's will. That effort is the subject of the present proceedings. . . .

The Lower Court's Order

In March 2002, a divided panel of the Court of Appeals . . . affirmed the District Court's determination that Sell was not dangerous. The majority noted that, according to the District Court, Sell's behavior at the Medical Center "amounted at most to an 'inappropriate familiarity and even infatuation' with a nurse." The Court of Appeals agreed, "[u]pon review," that "the evidence does not support a finding that Sell posed a danger to himself or others at the Medical Center."

The Court of Appeals also affirmed the District Court's order requiring medication in order to render Sell competent to stand trial. Focusing solely on the serious fraud charges, the panel majority concluded that the "government has an essential interest in bringing a defendant to trial." It added that the District Court "correctly concluded that there were no less intrusive means." After reviewing the conflicting views of the experts, the panel majority found antipsychotic drug treatment "medically appropriate" for Sell. It added that the "medical evidence presented indicated a reasonable probability that Sell will fairly be able to participate in his trial." One member of the panel dissented primarily on the ground that the fraud and money laundering charges were "not serious enough to warrant the forced medication of the defendant."

We granted certiorari [review] to determine whether the Eighth Circuit "erred in rejecting" Sell's argument that "allowing the government to administer antipsychotic medication against his will solely to render him competent to stand trial for non-violent offenses," violated the Constitution—in effect by improperly depriving Sell of an important "liberty" that the Constitution guarantees.

We first examine whether the Eighth Circuit had jurisdiction to decide Sell's appeal. The District Court's judgment, from which Sell had appealed, was a pretrial order. . . .

The law normally requires a defendant to wait until the end of the trial to obtain appellate review of a pretrial order. The relevant jurisdictional statute, authorizes federal courts of appeals to review "*final* decisions of the district courts." (Emphasis added.) And the term "final decision" normally refers to a final judgment, such as a judgment of guilt, that terminates a criminal proceeding.

Nonetheless, there are exceptions to this rule. . . .

The order (1) "conclusively determine[s] the disputed question," namely, whether Sell has a legal right to avoid forced medication. The order also (2) "resolve[s] an important issue," for, as this Court's cases make clear, involuntary medical treatment raises questions of clear constitutional importance. . . . At the same time, the basic issue—whether Sell must undergo medication against his will—is "completely separate from the merits of the action," *i.e.*, whether Sell is guilty or innocent of the crimes charged. The issue is wholly separate as well from questions concerning trial procedures. Finally, the issue is (3) "effectively unreviewable on appeal from a final judgment." By the time of trial Sell will have undergone forced medication—the very harm that he seeks to avoid. He cannot undo that harm even if he is acquitted. Indeed, if he is acquitted, there will be no appeal through which he might obtain review. . . .

We conclude that the District Court order from which Sell appealed was an appealable "collateral order." The Eighth Circuit had jurisdiction to hear the appeal. And we consequently have jurisdiction to decide the question presented, whether involuntary medication violates Sell's constitutional rights.

Constitutional Law Precedents

We turn now to the basic question presented: Does forced administration of antipsychotic drugs to render Sell competent to stand trial unconstitutionally deprive him of his "liberty" to reject medical treatment? Two prior precedents, set forth the framework for determining the legal answer. . . .

These two cases, *Washington v. Harper* and *Riggins v. Nevada*, indicate that the Constitution permits the Government involuntarily to administer antipsychotic drugs to a mentally ill defendant facing serious criminal charges in order to render that defendant competent to stand trial, but only if the treatment is medically appropriate, is substantially unlikely to have side effects that may undermine the fairness of the trial, and, taking account of less intrusive alternatives, is necessary significantly to further important governmental trial-related interests.

This standard will permit involuntary administration of drugs solely for trial competence purposes in certain instances. But those instances may be rare. That is because the standard says or fairly implies the following:

First, a court must find that *important* governmental interests are at stake. The Government's interest in bringing to trial an individual accused of a serious crime is important. That is so whether the offense is a serious crime against the person or a serious crime against property. In both instances the Government seeks to protect through application of the criminal law the basic human need for security.

Courts, however, must consider the facts of the individual case in evaluating the Government's interest in prosecution. Special circumstances may lessen the importance of that interest. The defendant's failure to take drugs voluntarily, for example, may mean lengthy confinement in an institution for the mentally ill—and that would diminish the risks that ordinarily attach to freeing without punishment one who has committed a serious crime. We do not mean to suggest that civil commitment is a substitute for a criminal trial. The Government has a substantial interest in timely prosecution. And it may be difficult or impossible to try a defendant who regains competence after years of commitment during which memories may fade and evidence may be lost. The potential for future confinement affects, but does not totally undermine, the strength of the need for prosecution. The same is true of the possibility that the defendant has already been confined for a significant amount of time (for which he would receive credit toward any sentence ultimately imposed). Moreover, the Government has a concomitant, constitutionally essential interest in assuring that the defendant's trial is a fair one.

Second, the court must conclude that involuntary medication will *significantly further* those concomitant state interests. It must find that administration of the drugs is substantially likely to render the defendant competent to stand trial. At the same time, it must find that administration of the drugs is substantially unlikely to have side effects that will interfere significantly with the defendant's ability to assist counsel in conducting a trial defense, thereby rendering the trial unfair.

Third, the court must conclude that involuntary medication is *necessary* to further those interests. The court must find that any alternative, less intrusive treatments are unlikely to achieve substantially the same results. And the court must consider less intrusive means for administering the drugs, *e.g.,* a court order to the defendant backed by the contempt power, before considering more intrusive methods.

Fourth, as we have said, the court must conclude that administration of the drugs is *medically appropriate, i.e.,* in the patient's best medical interest in light of his medical condition. The specific kinds of drugs at issue may matter here as elsewhere. Different kinds of antipsychotic drugs may produce different side effects and enjoy different levels of success.

Purpose of Medication

We emphasize that the court applying these standards is seeking to determine whether involuntary administration of drugs is necessary significantly to further a particular governmental interest, namely, the interest in rendering the defendant *competent to stand trial.* A court need not consider whether to allow forced medication for that kind of purpose, if forced medication is warranted for a *different purpose,* such as the purposes set out in *Harper* related to the individual's dangerousness, or purposes related to the individual's own interests where refusal to take drugs puts his health gravely at risk. There are often strong reasons for a court to determine whether forced administration of drugs can be justified on these alternative grounds *before* turning to the trial competence question. . . .

If a court authorizes medication on these alternative grounds, the need to consider authorization on trial competence grounds will likely disappear. Even if a court decides medication cannot be authorized on the alternative grounds, the findings underlying such a decision will help to inform expert opinion and judicial decision making in respect to a request to administer drugs for trial competence purposes. At the least, they will facilitate direct medical and legal focus upon such questions as: Why is it medically appropriate forcibly to administer antipsychotic drugs to an individual who

(1) is *not* dangerous *and* (2) *is* competent to make up his own mind about treatment? Can bringing such an individual to trial *alone* justify in whole (or at least in significant part) administration of a drug that may have adverse side effects, including side effects that may to some extent impair a defense at trial? We consequently believe that a court, asked to approve forced administration of drugs for purposes of rendering a defendant competent to stand trial, should ordinarily determine whether the Government seeks, or has first sought, permission for forced administration of drugs on these other *Harper*-type grounds; and, if not, why not.

When a court must nonetheless reach the trial competence question, the factors discussed above, should help it make the ultimate constitutionally required judgment. Has the Government, in light of the efficacy, the side effects, the possible alternatives, and the medical appropriateness of a particular course of antipsychotic drug treatment, shown a need for that treatment sufficiently important to overcome the individual's protected interest in refusing it? . . .

The Court of Appeals apparently agreed with the District Court that "Sell's inappropriate behavior . . . amounted at most to an 'inappropriate familiarity and even infatuation' with a nurse." That being so, it also agreed that "the evidence does not support a finding that Sell posed a danger to himself or others at the Medical Center. . . ."

We must assume that Sell was not dangerous. And on that hypothetical assumption, we find that the Court of Appeals was wrong to approve forced medication solely to render Sell competent to stand trial. For one thing, the Magistrate's opinion makes clear that he did *not* find forced medication legally justified on trial competence grounds alone. Rather, the Magistrate concluded that Sell *was* dangerous, and he wrote that forced medication was "the only way to render the defendant *not dangerous and* competent to stand trial."

Moreover, the record of the hearing before the Magistrate shows that the experts themselves focused mainly upon the dangerousness issue. Consequently the experts did not pose important questions—questions, for example, about trial-related side effects and risks—the answers to which could have helped determine whether forced medication was warranted on trial competence grounds alone. Rather, the Medical Center's experts conceded that their proposed medications had "significant" side effects and that "there has to be a cost benefit analysis." And in making their "cost-benefit" judgments, they primarily took into account Sell's dangerousness, not the need to bring him to trial.

The failure to focus upon trial competence could well have mattered. Whether a particular drug will tend to sedate a defendant, interfere with communication with counsel, prevent rapid reaction to trial developments, or diminish the ability to express emotions are matters important in determining the permissibility of medication to restore competence, but not necessarily relevant when dangerousness is primarily at issue. We cannot tell whether the side effects of antipsychotic medication were likely to undermine the fairness of a trial in Sell's case.

Finally, the lower courts did not consider that Sell has already been confined at the Medical Center for a long period of time, and that his refusal to take antipsychotic drugs might result in further lengthy confinement. Those factors, the first because a defendant ordinarily receives credit toward a sentence for time served, and the second because it reduces the likelihood of the defendant's committing future crimes, moderate—though they do not eliminate—the importance of the governmental interest in prosecution.

For these reasons, we believe that the present orders authorizing forced administration of antipsychotic drugs cannot stand.

> "The adverse effects of today's narrow holding are as nothing compared to the adverse effects of the new rule of law that underlies the holding."

Dissenting Opinion: The *Sell* Ruling Will Allow Criminal Defendants to Disrupt Trials Already in Progress

Antonin Scalia

Antonin Scalia became a justice of the U.S. Supreme Court in 1986. He is a strong conservative who believes in a strict interpretation of the Constitution, according to the meaning it had when originally adopted. The following viewpoint is an excerpt from his dissenting opinion in the case of Sell v. United States, in which the court ruled that a mentally ill defendant cannot be forcibly medicated for the sole purpose of standing trial except under special circumstances. Justice Scalia's objection to this ruling centers on the issue of allowing a defendant to appeal a court order for medication before the trial is over, which he considers contrary to the legal rules for appeals. This precedent, he asserts, will allow all criminal defendants to appeal court orders of any kind on grounds that their constitutional rights have been violated, thus holding up in-progress trials for months. In his opinion, neither the court of appeals nor the Supreme Court had jurisdiction in the case and therefore should not have decided it.

Antonin Scalia, dissenting opinion, *Charles Thomas Sell v. United States*, U.S. Supreme Court, June 16, 2003.

Today's narrow holding will allow criminal defendants in petitioner's position to engage in opportunistic behavior. They can, for example, voluntarily take their medication until halfway through trial, then abruptly refuse and demand an interlocutory appeal from the order that medication continue on a compulsory basis. This sort of concern for the disruption of criminal proceedings—strangely missing from the Court's discussion today—is what has led us to state many times that we interpret the collateral-order exception narrowly in criminal cases.

Ruling Will Allow Defendants to Hold Up Trials for Months

But the adverse effects of today's narrow holding are as nothing compared to the adverse effects of the new rule of law that underlies the holding. The Court's opinion announces that appellate jurisdiction is proper because review after conviction and sentence will come only after "Sell will have undergone forced medication—the very harm that he seeks to avoid." This analysis effects a breathtaking expansion of appellate jurisdiction over interlocutory orders. If it is applied faithfully (and some appellate panels will be eager to apply it faithfully), any criminal defendant who asserts that a trial court order will, if implemented, cause an immediate violation of his constitutional (or perhaps even statutory?) rights may immediately appeal. He is empowered to hold up the trial for months by claiming that review after final judgment "would come too late" to prevent the violation. A trial-court order requiring the defendant to wear an electronic bracelet could be attacked as an immediate infringement of the constitutional right to "bodily integrity"; an order refusing to allow the defendant to wear a T-shirt that says "Black Power" in front of the jury could be attacked as an immediate violation of First Amendment rights; and an order compelling testimony could be attacked as an immediate denial of Fifth

Amendment rights. All these orders would be immediately appealable. *Flanagan* and *Carroll*, which held that appellate review of orders that might infringe a defendant's constitutionally protected rights *still* had to wait until final judgment, are seemingly overruled. The narrow gate of entry to the collateral-order doctrine—hitherto traversable by only (1) orders unreviewable on appeal from judgment and (2) orders denying an asserted right not to be tried—has been generously widened. . . .

Petitioner could have obtained pre-trial review of the medication order by filing suit under the Administrative Procedure Act, or even by filing a *Bivens v. Six Unknown Fed. Narcotics Agents* action, which is available to federal pretrial detainees challenging the conditions of their confinement. In such a suit, he could have obtained immediate appellate review of denial of relief. But if he chooses to challenge his forced medication in the context of a criminal trial, he must abide by the limitations attached to such a challenge—which prevent him from stopping the proceedings in their tracks. Petitioner's mistaken litigation strategy, and this Court's desire to decide an interesting constitutional issue, do not justify a disregard of the limits that Congress has imposed on courts of appeals' (and our own) jurisdiction. We should vacate the judgment here, and remand the case to the Court of Appeals with instructions to dismiss.

"The Court was hedging its bets when it should have come out forcefully with a prohibition on forcible medication of a mentally ill defendant solely to make him competent for trial."

The *Sell* Ruling Did Not Go Far Enough in Protecting the Constitutional Liberty of Mentally Ill Defendants

John R. Hayes

John R. Hayes was a law student at Northwestern University at the time he wrote this viewpoint. In it, he argues that in the case of Sell v. United States, the Supreme Court did not go far enough in protecting the rights of mentally ill criminal defendants. He points out that the constitutional right of such defendants to be free from unwanted psychiatric medication was clearly stated in opinions in previous cases, and that this right is not outweighed by the government's interest in bringing criminals to trial. Moreover, the harmful side effects of psychiatric drugs interfere with the defendant's ability to receive a fair trial. The Court in Sell dismissed these effects, which Hayes believes was a serious mistake. Finally, in his opinion, it did not give sufficient weight to the issue of whether Sell's crimes were serious enough to justify forcibly medicating him solely for trial purposes. Although it re-

John R. Hayes, "*Sell v. United States*: Is Competency Enough to Forcibly Medicate a Criminal Defendant?" *Journal of Criminal Law and Criminology*, vol. 94, Spring 2004, pp. 674–683. Copyright © 2004 by Northwestern University, School of Law. Reprinted by special permission of Northwestern University School of Law, *The Journal of Law and Criminology*.

fused to authorize medication in his case, its failure to distinguish fraud from murder set a dangerous precedent that will affect the rights of other defendants.

A n individual's constitutionally protected "liberty interest" to be free from forcible medication has been recognized in all Supreme Court cases dealing with the issue. The Court in *Harper* stated that an individual has a significant and constitutionally protected "liberty interest" in avoiding the forcible administration of antipsychotic drugs. In *Riggins*, the Court found that the trial court's failure to consider the defendant's liberty interest in being free from unwanted antipsychotic medication might have impaired the constitutionally protected rights invoked by the defendant. Though the Court has split on when this liberty interest is outweighed by a legitimate, important, and essential state interest—outweighed in *Harper*, not outweighed in *Riggins*—the clear implication from the Court is that this liberty interest will always outweigh the governmental interest of rendering a defendant competent to stand trial.

Constitutional Basis for an Individual's Liberty Interest

The Fifth Amendment of the United States Constitution specifically provides that an individual in a criminal case may not be deprived of liberty without due process of law. Similarly, the Fourteenth Amendment of the United States Constitution prohibits the states from depriving *any person* of liberty without due process of law. . . .

Courts have explicitly recognized that a criminal defendant awaiting trial has a substantive due process right to refuse the administering of antipsychotic drugs. . . .

In addition to a substantive due process right, courts have recognized a procedural due process right for criminal defendants that must be met in order to involuntarily medicate them with antipsychotic drugs to render them competent to stand trial. This procedural due process right was laid out clearly in *Sell*. The *Sell* Court found that the Due Process Clause of the Fifth Amendment permits the government to involuntarily administer antipsychotic drugs to a mentally ill defendant facing serious criminal charges to render him competent to stand trial. The test posited in *Sell* assumed the government's right to forcibly medicate a pretrial detainee but laid out substantial limitations. In so doing, the Court failed to recognize that the substantive due process rights of an individual should actually override the state's interest in rendering a defendant competent to stand trial, regardless of whether the procedural due process rights were met or not. . . .

While the Court in *Harper* authorized forcible medication of an *inmate*, it was Justice [John Paul] Stevens's dissent in *Harper* that addressed the importance of an individual's liberty interest in light of the possibility of forcible medication of antipsychotic drugs. He stated that every violation of a person's bodily integrity is an invasion of that person's liberty. He further emphasized the invasion of an individual's liberty when the intrusion involves a substantial risk of permanent injury and premature death, as is the case with antipsychotic drugs. Justice Stevens also focused on the mind-altering properties of the drugs and on the fact that this constituted a deprivation of liberty in "the most literal and fundamental sense." Justice Stevens's dissent carries even more weight when viewed in the context of *Harper*. *Harper* involved the forcible administration of antipsychotic drugs to a mentally ill *inmate*. It can be reasonably argued that an inmate's liberty interest is substantially less than that of a pretrial detainee who is presumed innocent. Thus, Justice Stevens was correct in concluding that "the liberty of citizens to resist the administration of mind altering drugs arises from our Nation's most basic values. . . ."

An Individual's Liberty Interest Outweighs Any Governmental Interest

A mentally ill defendant found incompetent to stand trial does not run free in society. There are strict guidelines and regulations governing civil commitment, along with continuous treatment and psychiatric review. In light of these circumstances, it is clear that an individual's liberty interest outweighs the governmental interest to bring a criminal defendant to trial.

This point goes to the underlying rationale behind the test laid out in *Sell:* in order to involuntarily administer antipsychotic medication to a criminal defendant the state must show that such medication is *necessary* to further important government related trial-interests. Again, Justice Stevens's dissenting opinion in *Harper* provides a clear analysis of the balancing involved in authorizing forcible administration of antipsychotic drugs to an individual. While Justice Stevens's dissent did not deal with trial-interests, it did examine the balancing of liberty interests with state institutional concerns. He concluded that the majority allowed the exaggerated response of involuntary administration of antipsychotic drugs on the basis of purely institutional concerns, thus creating a "muddled rationale." While the state's interest in running a safe and secure prison—and also in bringing a defendant to trial—is clearly both *legitimate* and *important*, it is not clear that a violation of an individual's liberty interest through forcible medication is *necessary* to further those interests.

In conclusion, an individual's liberty interest to avoid unwanted administration of mind-altering drugs is deeply rooted in the Constitution. Both the Fifth and Fourteenth Amendments guarantee that an individual not be deprived of liberty through due process of law. An individual's bodily integrity is a part of this liberty interest. While the government does have a legitimate interest in bringing the accused to trial, this interest is not strong enough to ignore an individual's right to avoid state-imposed medication that will alter her mind and will. . . .

An Individual's Right to a Fair Trial Is Undermined by Involuntary Administration of Antipsychotic Medication

A defendant's right to a fair and just trial becomes an issue when the defendant's competency to stand trial is questioned. A defendant's right to a fair trial is jeopardized when antipsychotic medication is administered involuntarily to a defendant solely to render him competent to stand trial. . . . A defendant rendered competent through chemistry is at a serious disadvantage, in that their ability to communicate and assist in their defense is severely limited. The potential harmful side effects of antipsychotic drugs puts the criminal defendant forcibly medicated with such drugs at a serious disadvantage. . . .

The ability of a defendant to actively participate in the trial, if she so chooses, is a fundamental and constitutionally protected right of a criminal defendant. The potential side effects of antipsychotic drugs can have a significant impact on a defendant's right to a fair trial. Justice Kennedy's concurring opinion in *Riggins* explored this issue in detail. . . .

These elementary protections against state intrusion require that the state in every case make a showing that there is no significant risk that the drugs would impair or alter the defendant's ability to react to the testimony at trial or to interact with his counsel on behalf of his defense.

The side effects of antipsychotic drugs can significantly affect the defendant's demeanor and cognitive functions during a trial. Justice Kennedy found that these drugs could prejudice a defendant in two possible ways. First, they could alter his or her demeanor in a manner that would prejudice his or her reactions in the courtroom, and second, the drugs could render him or her unable and unwilling to effectively assist counsel in the defense. . . .

The Court in *Sell*, while recognizing the effect of antipsychotic drugs on a defendant's demeanor and cognitive abilities, failed to find that these side effects were significant enough to *always* hinder a defendant's right to a fair trial. This terse dismissal of the side effects of antipsychotic drugs is one of the major flaws with the Court's opinion. It was unwilling to take the extra, bold step necessary to bring the law in line with medicine. These drugs are not perfect and have serious consequences that significantly undermine a defendant's right to a fair trial. The American Psychiatric Association stated in *Riggins*:

> By administering medication, the State may be creating a prejudicial negative demeanor in the defendant—making him look nervous, restless . . . or so calm or sedated as to appear bored, cold, unfeeling, and unresponsive. . . . That such effects may be subtle does not make them any less real or potentially influential.

The fact that the medical community recognizes such a prejudice should serve as a clear announcement to the Court that antipsychotic medication is unpredictable and complex and consequently should not be relied on to create the perfect, competent defendant.

Justice Kennedy pointed out in *Riggins* that there existed a difference between competency to stand trial and the purpose of involuntary medication in *Harper*, which was to halt the dangerousness of an incarcerated individual to himself and others. In *Sell*, the Court . . . made strong overtures that a trial court should focus on dangerousness when considering involuntary medication of a defendant, as evidenced by its strict standard for medicating solely for competence. The Court was hedging its bets when it should have come out forcefully with a prohibition on forcible medication of a mentally ill defendant solely to make him competent for trial.

In sum, an individual has a constitutionally protected right to a fair trial. An individual's competency is an essential aspect of this right. Consequently, if the state compels the individual to involuntarily take antipsychotic medication it is significantly hindering the ability of a defendant to assist in his or her defense and thus have a fair trial. . . .

In failing to adopt a standard prohibiting forcible medication of a mentally ill defendant with antipsychotic drugs for the sole purpose of rendering him competent to stand trial, the Court missed an opportunity to align this area soundly with the Constitution.

The Court Extended Its Standard of Seriousness of the Crime Too Far

The test laid out by the Court in *Sell* allowed the government to involuntarily administer antipsychotic drugs to a mentally ill defendant facing *serious* criminal charges. If one admits that the Court was correct in formulating such a test, there still remains the glaring issue of whether Sell's alleged crimes were serious. . . .

The sentencing guidelines for crimes against property could provide a solid bright line test as to whether the crime reaches the level of serious. The Court should have defined this line and clearly stated that based on the sentencing guidelines, crimes of fraud do not reach the level of seriousness that would allow for a violation of an individual's liberty interest. . . .

The above facts clearly distinguish *Sell* from *Riggins*, a case in which the defendant was accused of murder. It can be legitimately argued that the State has a strong and essential interest in bringing an accused murderer to trial. . . . However, when the crime is one solely involving property, that essential interest lessens and the individual's liberty interest cannot be ignored. An individual's right to bodily integrity and to be free from intrusion is a sacred right and crimes such as wire fraud and money-laundering, which are crimes that need to be punished, do not warrant pushing aside that right. . . . The possible debilitating and life-long side effects, along with the impairing of a right to a fair trial, do not justify the forcible medication of an individual to further the state's interest.

In conclusion, it was error for the Court in *Sell* to use the seriousness of the crimes in *Riggins* as a basis for the test used in *Sell*. Although the Court refused to uphold the authorization of antipsychotic drugs in both cases, it set out a dangerous precedent. Theoretically, an individual could be forcibly medicated with antipsychotic drugs to become competent to stand trial for nonviolent crimes involving such limited punishment as thirty-three months in prison. The "seriousness of the crime standard" laid out by the Court in *Sell* significantly curtails the liberty interest of an individual to be free from any unwanted bodily intrusion and deprives a defendant of a right to a fair trial.

" Sell v. United States *represents a sea-change for how the question of involuntary medication of defendants must be handled.*"

The *Sell* Ruling Will Result in Major Changes in How Involuntary Medication of Mentally Ill Defendants Is Handled

Brett Trowbridge

Brett Trowbridge, a forensic psychologist and lawyer, is the executive director of the Trowbridge Foundation. In the following viewpoint, he explains that because in Sell v. United States *the routine forcible medication of mentally ill criminal defendants was ruled unconstitutional, there must be significant changes in how such cases are handled. Although in some cases a psychiatrist will still be able to order involuntary medication, in others a court will need to decide whether the case is important enough for it to be justified. Trowbridge states that this will require a hearing with the defendant present; if indigent, he will have to be provided with counsel and expert witnesses. The defense will need to ask that many factors in the case be reviewed by a psychologist or psychiatrist, and the prosecution will need to be sure that all these factors have been mentioned to ensure that, if a court order for forced medication is issued, it will withstand appeal.*

Brett Trowbridge, "Medicating Incompetent Defendants Against Their Will to Restore Competency: *Sell v. United States* Changes Current Practice," The Trowbridge Foundation, November, 2003. www.trowbridgefoundation.org/docs/medicating.htm. Reproduced by permission.

When I began working at the forensic unit at Western State Hospital in the late 1970s, defendants committed to the hospital for 15-day evaluations for assessment of their competency to stand trial were routinely medicated with antipsychotic drugs involuntarily even before a judicial determination was made as to their competency to stand trial. Indeed, when notified by a jail that a psychotic patient was being transported to the hospital, Western State Hospital staff was routinely instructed to meet the new patient at the door with a loaded syringe.

Medications were given involuntarily whenever the ward psychiatrist ordered them and in whatever dosages he deemed appropriate. No special procedures or hearings were required beforehand, even in cases involving relatively minor crimes. In most cases once the medications took effect the patients became more rational and were deemed to be competent to stand trial. Just as occurs now, defendants routinely were involuntarily medicated right up until or even during their trials.

Decisions by the U.S. Supreme Court have clarified that such practices are unconstitutional. Indeed, in a very recent decision the Supreme Court has imposed important new requirements. This case, *Sell v. United States*, represents a sea-change for how the question of involuntary medication of defendants must be handled in Washington courts. . . .

Sell v. United States

[In] *Sell v. United States*, decided June 16, 2003, the U.S. Supreme Court has clearly addressed what factors need to be considered on the record before a defendant can be medicated against his will in order to render him competent to stand trial. . . .

The U.S. Supreme Court granted certiorari [agreed to review the case] to determine whether the Eighth Circuit erred in rejecting Sell's argument that allowing the government to administer anti-psychotic medication against his will solely to render him competent to stand trial violated the constitution. Justice [Stephen] Breyer wrote the opinion for the six-justice majority, with [Antonin] Scalia, [Clarence] Thomas and [Sandra Day] O'Connor dissenting.

Breyer, citing *Harper* and *Riggins*, stated that "the Constitution permits the government involuntarily to administer anti-psychotic drugs to a mentally ill defendant facing serious criminal charges in order to render that defendant competent to stand trial, but only if the treatment is medically appropriate, is substantially unlikely to have side-effects that may undermine the fairness of the trial, and, taking into account of less intrusive alternatives is necessary significantly to further important governmental trial-related interests." This standard would permit involuntary administration of such drugs solely for trial competence purposes in certain instances, but, as Breyer noted, those instances may be rare for four reasons.

First, a court must find that important government interests are at stake—that is, it must consider whether the defendant who is not brought to trial would likely remain in a mental institution, and/or whether the defendant who had already spent such a large amount of time in a mental institution would, if convicted, likely be sentenced to time served.

Second, the court must conclude that involuntary medication will significantly further concomitant state interests. Administration of the drugs must be substantially likely to render the defendant competent to stand trial and, at the same time, be substantially unlikely to have side effects interfering significantly with the defendant's ability to assist counsel in conducting a trial defense.

Involuntary Medication Must Be Necessary

Third, the court must conclude that involuntary medication is necessary to further these interests. Any alternative, less intrusive treatments must be unlikely to achieve substantially the same results. And less intrusive means for administering the drugs must be considered—e.g., a court order to the defendant backed by the contempt power—before employing more intrusive methods.

Fourth, the court must conclude that administration of the drugs is medically appropriate, i.e., in the patient's best medical interest in light of his medical condition.

Before a court decides to order involuntary administration of medications solely to render the defendant competent to stand trial, it should first decide whether "forced medication is warranted for any different purpose, such as the purposes set forth in *Harper* related to the individual's dangerousness, or purposes related to the individual's own interests where refusal to take drugs put his health gravely at risk." Thus, Breyer seems to be saying that civil commitment should be considered as a less restrictive alternative.

Both the district court and the Eighth Circuit had concluded that Sell was not dangerous to himself or others in the institutional setting and had rested their decision to allow forced medication solely on trial competency grounds. At the hearing before the magistrate, however, the experts had focused mainly on the dangerousness issue. Breyer noted that this failure to focus upon trial competence could well have mattered, because the effects of medication upon the defendant are matters important in determining the permissibility of medication.

Breyer's final point was that the lower courts did not consider that Sell has already been confined at the Medical Center for a long period of time, and that his refusal to take antipsychotic drugs might result in further lengthy confinement. The case was remanded for further proceedings consistent with the opinion.

Implications of the Decision

It seems clear that in some cases such as *Harper* decision as to forced medication can be made by a psychiatrist instead of a judge. In other cases in which the sole argument is that involuntary medication is necessary to render the defendant competent to stand trial, a judicial hearing will be required, for the *Sell* criteria are mostly legal, not medical in nature.

The court will have to decide whether the case is important enough that forced medication can be justified. Misdemeanors and minor felonies will probably not qualify, especially if the defendant has already been incarcerated on the charge for any substantial period. The court will then have to hear expert testimony on the following issues:

1. Whether the specific medication proposed at the specific dosage proposed is likely to restore the defendant's competency to stand trial.

2. Whether the side-effects of that specific medication at that dosage will interfere significantly with the defendant's ability to assist counsel under the facts of the case as charged.

3. Whether any alternative, less intrusive treatments could likely restore competency, including ordering the defendant to take the drugs under threat of contempt.

4. Whether the specific drug proposed is medically appropriate.

5. Whether there exist any other ways of allowing forced medication, including civil commitment and/or the appointment of a guardian.

6. Whether the need for involuntary medication is sufficiently important to overcome the individual's protected interest in refusing it in light of factors relevant to this particular defendant such as his religious beliefs and his approach to medical treatment in general.

Given the complexity of the criteria to be considered, it would seem unlikely that any court would find that the defendant can be forced to go through such a hearing without representation by counsel. Further, it would seem that the defendant would have to be present for the hearing so that the court would have an opportunity to consider his demeanor and appearance and any testimony he cared to give, although he would undoubtedly retain the right to remain silent. It seems obvious, moreover, that the defendant, if indigent, would have to be provided services of expert witnesses to challenge the testimony of government witnesses, and that the rules of evidence would have to apply. Finally, because it is clear that the defendant would have the right to appeal, the court's decision would have to be written, and all the *Sell* factors would have to be mentioned in that decision.

Changes from Current Procedure

Such hearings will be a significant departure from current practice in Washington. Before *Sell* if the state hospital found that a defendant was incompetent to stand trial, it would ask in its formal report to the trial court that it be given permission to medicate the defendant involuntarily. Generally the specific medication and dosage proposed was not set forth.

Although sometimes hearings occurred at which expert testimony was offered, rarely did defense experts participate in such hearings. Indeed, usually there was not a hearing, as the defense attorney typically waived the hearing on behalf of the presumably incompetent defendant and stipulated to any order requiring forced medication. Under *Sell* such procedure will not pass constitutional muster unless the defendant himself agrees to take medication voluntarily.

Finally, the amount of time already served or likely to be served has not previously been taken into account.

In this post-*Sell* era defense lawyers should meet stats hospital requests for permission to involuntarily medicate by asking for the appointment of an expert psychologist or psychiatrist whenever the defendant found incompetent is resisting the taking of anti-psychotic medication.

That expert would review records to determine whether the drug proposed at the dosage proposed had been documented to be effective in the past in restoring rationality and/or determine whether other less restrictive means could restore competency. The expert would research potential side effects of the medication at the proposed dosage. Indeed, the expert would address whether the drug could sedate the defendant, interfere with his communication with counsel, prevent rapid reaction to trial developments, or diminish the ability to express emotions.

The expert would have access to the state hospital chart to review whether civil commitment and/or guardianship had been attempted. The expert could testify as to what the likely consequences would be of dismissal, i.e., whether the defendant would likely remain in the hospital anyway.

The expert would also address the "seriousness" of the alleged offense and look at what the likely sentence would be if the defendant were medicated involuntarily, found competent and convicted.

It would be the prosecution's job to see to it that all of these factors were mentioned in any order the court issued allowing forced medication, so that the order would withstand appeal.

> "By allowing the 'dangerousness' ambi-
> guity in its careful articulation of what
> is necessary for a mentally ill defen-
> dant to receive a fair trial, the Court
> provided an easy way for prosecutors to
> succeed in a motion for forced medica-
> tion."

The *Sell* Ruling Will Have Little Effect Because Defendants Can Still Be Forcibly Medicated if Called Dangerous

Kelly Hilgers and Paula Ramer

Kelly Hilgers and Paula Ramer were law students at Georgetown University Law Center at the time this viewpoint was written. In it, they discuss the difficulties faced by defense attorneys in deciding whether to contest the prosecution's desire for involuntary medication of criminal defendants. In some cases, an attorney may feel that a mentally ill client needs medication, even though it will mean that he or she is forced to stand trial. On the other hand, psychiatric medication often has serious side effects that are extremely unpleasant and that would make it difficult for the defendant to participate in his or her own defense or to present him- or herself favorably to a jury, so the resulting trial might not be fair. Furthermore, say Hilgers and Ramer, the Supreme Court's Sell v. United States *decision may not have much*

Kelly Hilgers and Paula Ramer, "Forced Medication of Defendants to Achieve Trial Competency: An Update on the Law After *Sell*," *Georgetown Journal of Legal Ethics*, vol. 17, Summer 2004, pp. 813–826. Copyright © 2004. Reprinted with permission of the publisher, *Georgetown Journal of Legal Ethics*.

practical effect because its protection of the constitutional right to avoid unwanted medication does not apply if a mentally ill defendant is called dangerous.

An attorney representing a defendant who is or may be mentally incompetent faces a series of ethical dilemmas. First, the attorney may have to ascertain whether her client is, in fact, mentally incompetent, without revealing that client's confidential information and while protecting the attorney-client relationship. The attorney will then have to balance her client's need for treatment against the possibility that such treatment may make her client competent to stand trial. In order to protect her client from legal harm, she may have to argue her client's right to live in a delusional state, even when the client desperately needs antipsychotic medication. Conversely, a prosecutor may find herself representing a defendant's medical interests so that she can proceed with the prosecution. Dealing with a mentally incompetent defendant places attorneys in precarious ethical positions. These issues came to light in the Supreme Court's recent decision, *Sell v. United States*. . . .

Prior to *Sell*, it was well-established doctrine that an incompetent defendant could not be tried or convicted of a crime. The Supreme Court's previous cases had failed to clarify, however, how far a court might go to restore the trial competency of a mentally ill defendant. . . .

Implications of *Sell*

The ruling in *Sell* has produced mixed reviews. Some commentators [David Hudson Jr.] argue that "[t]he court's opinion makes it harder procedurally for the government to establish before a court that the medication will not impair a criminal defendant," thus making it more difficult for the government to involuntarily medicate defendants, and allowing incompetent defendants a greater chance of avoiding trial. Another observer [John Parry] has said that the ruling strikes an "intermediate position," creating a "substantial hurdle." A *Washington Post* editorial applauded the decision, writing, "a patient's medical care should never be made to serve the retributive needs of the criminal justice system." These critics feel the decision in *Sell* marks a sharp shift from the Court's previous holdings in *Harper* and *Riggins.*

However, other critics of the *Sell* decision argue that it did not go far enough to protect the rights of mentally incompetent defendants and in fact, changes little. As one legal scholar [Tamar Meekins] puts it, "it seems that the court has avoided a turn to the left on this important issue of defendants' rights." One concern is that the ruling allows a defendant to be forcibly medicated for reasons other than competency, thus ignoring the defendant's procedural right to a fair trial:

> As balanced a test as [the *Sell* standard] seems, the court expressly limited its use to situations where the government seeks to restore a defendant's mental competency. In so doing, it created a loophole. Now, it's possible that lower courts can allow defendants to be medicated on another ground— that they are dangerous to themselves or to others. That means that the essential constitutional rights of pretrial defendants may still remain in jeopardy.

Thus, *Sell* leaves open the possibility that a defendant may be medicated for his alleged dangerousness and be forced to stand trial without taking account of the factors listed in *Sell* to ensure that none of his procedural rights are violated. . . .

The Court in [*United States v.*] *Colon* found it unnecessary to administer the *Sell* test when the defendant was found to be a danger to himself or others. This type of analysis may prove to undermine the efficacy of the Court's decision in *Sell* by allowing courts to forcibly medicate defendants without taking into account possible effects on their participation at trial. It will be up to the defendant's lawyers to consider such possibilities in deciding whether or not it is in the client's best interests to contest a motion for involuntary medication. . . .

Finding a Defendant Mentally Incompetent

The first question an attorney faces is deciding whether her client is mentally incompetent, an issue which may not always be clear to a person with no medical training or diagnostic experience. . . .

A recent ABA [American Bar Association] Opinion provides some clarification of situations in which an attorney finds herself representing a potentially incompetent defendant. . . . In theory, an attorney should be able to consult with a doctor regarding her client's mental incompetence.

However, the opinion's encouragement to seek help is counterbalanced by its repeated warnings to attorneys to keep in mind the client's own desires and autonomy. A lawyer may take protective action in dealing with a potentially incompetent client, but it "should be the least restrictive under the circumstances." For example, the opinion warns against the appointment of a guardian unless absolutely necessary, noting that such an appointment "is a serious deprivation of the client's rights and ought not be undertaken if other, less drastic, solutions are available." The opinion goes on to state:

> A client who is making decisions that the lawyer considers to be ill-considered is not necessarily unable to act in his own interest, and the lawyer should not seek protective action merely to protect the client from what the lawyer believes are errors in judgment. . . .

The attorney must attempt to differentiate between errors in judgment and mental illness. Can a lawyer make this distinction between eccentricity and true mental illness? Should she? These questions are likely to present an attorney in this situation with a number of difficult decisions.

The problems discussed above present preliminary issues before a defendant is declared incompetent. Once a defendant's mental incompetence has been established, an attorney faces a new set of issues. In a situation where a mentally disabled client has refused to take medication to improve his competence, a lawyer has two choices: to contest the government's motion or to accede to it. Each of these choices has its own set of issues.

Contesting the Government's Motion

Model Rule [of Professional Conduct] 1.2 requires a lawyer to "abide by a client's desires concerning the objectives of representation . . . and . . . consult with the client as to the means by which they are to be pursued." This would seem to support an advocacy model of representation in which the lawyer follows the wishes of her client in all situations. This model presents a simple solution for the lawyer deciding whether or not to contest the government's motion for forced medication: because the client doesn't want the medication, the attorney should contest the motion. However, this model has received strong criticism from both the legal and medical communities. . . .

When a mentally ill client makes a questionable choice, it becomes the attorney's duty to determine whether or not that choice is in the client's best interests.

How then to determine whether defending a client's liberty interest in being free from forcibly administered medication is indeed in that client's best interests? Medical experts have questioned the choice to allow a mentally incompetent defendant to go without psychotropic drugs. . . .

The cost of leaving a sick individual to face his mental illness alone, without medication, can be high. The individual may suffer more from his illness than he would from being incarcerated. For example, without medication, the illness may progress to the point where the defendant is completely incapacitated. In addition, the individual may face indefinite civil commitment without the possibility of a trial. The attorney

must address the question of whether a mentally-ill client who rejects medication may have a better quality of life when taking it. . . .

However, the choice to give a client psychotropic drugs against his will is not as simple as it may seem. There are several questions that an attorney may have to answer before she can in good conscience allow the government to force medication upon her client. First, is it clear that the medication will actually ameliorate the client's illness and improve his quality of life? Second, how will the medication affect the client's legal proceedings?

It is sometimes unclear whether psychotropic drugs actually help to improve psychotic illnesses, or whether it merely tranquilizes the individual to the point where the problematic symptoms do not manifest themselves. Antipsychotic drugs tend to undermine an individual's will, making him more receptive to outside suggestion and instruction. . . .

At the same time, these drugs do not necessarily have a curative effect on long-term mental illnesses such as schizophrenia. It is thus difficult to decide whether medication simply calms the individual and makes him easier to manage, thus undermining his valuable interest in self-autonomy, or whether the medication will actually help cure the patient's illness.

Psychotropic medications are also known to have several sometimes serious and unpleasant side-effects. . . .

An attorney may reasonably question whether an individual who does not wish to be medicated, and who experiences such serious side effects, has a better quality of life with the drugs or without. . . .

Decisions During Trial

Some of the same side effects that make antipsychotic medication such an unpleasant experience can also make it difficult for the lawyer to follow the directive of the *Model Rules* and

consult with the client.... As *Sell* recognizes, the administration of antipsychotic drugs may make it more, not less, difficult for an incompetent client to participate.

For example, a client suffering from akathisia, or motor restlessness, may be so impatient that he cannot concentrate enough to consult with his lawyer. Alternatively, antipsychotic drugs, as noted before, can have a tranquilizing effect on the patient that produce "a psychological state of unusual receptiveness to the directions of custodians." Therefore, when a client agrees with his attorney to pursue a particular line of defense, it can be unclear whether it is the client or the drugs who is consenting to the strategy. Medication can also flatten an individual's will to the point of losing the desire of self-preservation. In the latter case, a drugged defendant may not care enough about his own well-being to participate in his defense at trial.

An added complication stems from the fact that a client who is suffering from side effects such as apathy or lack of spontaneity will often deny that there is any problem.... Thus the client's ability to participate in his own defense may be hampered, rather than aided, by psychotropic medication....

As Tamar Meekins writes:

> Many practicing trial lawyers have noted that defendants who are on such drugs as Melaril, Elavil and Valium may appear to be "out of it." I have had several clients who were restless, pacing back and forth, not motivated, constantly forgetful, constantly rocking back and forth, anxious, falling asleep, and seemingly unaware of the events happening around them, even in the courtroom.... Additionally, a defendant's affect, demeanor, and responsiveness are so compromised by some of these drugs that jurors and judges may ascribe negative connotations to the behavior that they observe in the courtroom. This works to compromise the defendant's credibility and presumption of innocence at trial.

When a defendant appears to be apathetic or uncaring about the crime that he is charged with, the jury may be apt to punish him more harshly. . . .

The holding in *Sell* provides little help for attorneys who are seeking to represent their mentally ill clients in the best possible fashion. The Supreme Court listed strict conditions that must be met in order for courts to forcibly medicate defendants in order to make them competent for trial. These conditions were meant to ensure that the liberty interests of mentally ill individuals are protected, and that they receive a fair trial. However, *Sell* allows forced medication under less strict conditions when defendants are adjudged to be dangerous to themselves or others. It is thus unclear whether *Sell* will have much of an effect at all. By allowing the "dangerousness" ambiguity in its careful articulation of what is necessary for a mentally ill defendant to receive a fair trial, the Court provided an easy way for prosecutors to succeed in a motion for forced medication.

Thus, it continues to be the responsibility of the defendant's attorney to determine whether such forced medication will, on balance, help or hurt her client, both medically speaking, and at trial. This judgment will involve balancing complicated factual issues, specific to the client and the case. It is a heavy responsibility to bear.

CHAPTER 4

Denying the Right of Terminally Ill Persons to Use Experimental Drugs

Case Overview

Abigail Alliance for Better Access to Developmental Drugs v. Andrew von Eschenbach (2007)

When Abigail Burroughs was only nineteen, she was diagnosed with a form of cancer that rarely occurs in young people. Her doctor, a prominent oncologist, thought that a new drug, Erbitux®, might save her life. Erbitux®, however, was still undergoing clinical trials and the Food and Drug Administration (FDA) had not approved it for use. Abigail was not eligible to participate in the trials because of particular factors in her case, and it was illegal for the manufacturer to provide experimental drugs directly to patients. Her parents tried for many months to find a way around the law, but they were unsuccessful. She died in 2001, at the age of twenty-one.

Soon after Abigail's death, her father founded a nonprofit advocacy group, the Abigail Alliance for Better Access to Developmental Drugs, to work toward change in the law. It has lobbied members of Congress and the FDA, trying to convince them that no patient should have to die merely because official approval of a promising new drug is years away. The FDA, however, maintains that experimental drugs are dangerous. The reason they are unapproved is that they are not known to be effective or even safe; they are by no means guaranteed to save lives, and may instead do harm. The Alliance argues that patients understand this and that the decision to try a risky treatment should lie with the person whose life is at stake, not with the government.

In 2003, having failed to get a law passed that would require the FDA to let terminally ill patients use new drugs prior to their approval, the Alliance filed suit in federal court on the grounds that the restriction on drug use by these patients was unconstitutional. The Constitution, it argued, embodies a right to make every attempt to save one's own life. The District Court disagreed, but on appeal, a three-member panel of the Circuit Court ruled that such a right does indeed exist. This ruling proved controversial, so it was set aside and the case was considered by the full Circuit Court. The viewpoints included in this chapter concern the Circuit Court's final decision in August, 2007, which held that there is no right to use drugs—even for the purpose of saving one's life—implied by the Constitution.

It is important to understand that the question before the court was not whether it is good or bad for terminally ill patients to have access to experimental drugs, but whether the Constitution *requires* that they be given access. If the use of unapproved drugs in the attempt to save one's own life is a constitutional right, it does not matter what effect such use has on society, although there was often confusion about this distinction in comments about the case. On the other hand, if the Constitution does not guarantee that right, the FDA's regulations concerning experimental drugs cannot be altered by a lawsuit—only legislation can overrule them.

The court was divided in its opinion. The two majority members of the panel that originally ruled in favor of the Alliance had not changed their minds, so Judge Judith Rogers wrote a dissenting opinion in which she was joined by Chief Judge Douglas Ginsburg. The Alliance appealed the decision to the U.S. Supreme Court, but the Supreme Court has time to consider only a small fraction of the cases that are presented to it. In January 2008, it declined to review this one, thereby allowing the Circuit Court's decision to stand.

> *"The Alliance has not provided evidence*
> *of a right to procure and use experi-*
> *mental drugs that is deeply rooted in*
> *our Nation's history and traditions."*

The Circuit Court's Decision: Terminally Ill Patients Do Not Have a Constitutional Right to Use Unapproved Drugs

Thomas B. Griffith

Thomas B. Griffith has been a federal judge on the United States Court of Appeals for the District of Columbia Circuit since 2005. He was previously General Counsel for Brigham Young Univer-sity. The following is his presentation of the majority opinion in the case of Abigail Alliance for Better Access to Developmental Drugs v. von Eschenbach, *in which the Court of Appeals ruled that terminally ill patients do not have a constitutional right to use experimental drugs that have not been approved by the FDA. In it, he considers the arguments presented by the Abigail Alliance and concludes, on the basis of past Supreme Court deci-sions and other precedents, that they are not valid. The Consti-tution does not confer any right that overrides governmental regulation of drugs. He says, however, a new balance between the risks and benefits of unproven drugs could be established through legislation, rather than by the courts.*

Thomas B. Griffith, majority opinion, *Abigail Alliance for Better Access to Developmen-tal Drugs v. Andrew von Eschenbach*, United States Court of Appeals for the District of Columbia Circuit, August 7, 2007, pp. 2–36. http://pacer.cadc.uscourts.gov/docs/common/opinions/200708/04-5350c.pdf.

This case presents the question whether the Constitution provides terminally ill patients a right of access to experimental drugs that have passed limited safety trials but have not been proven safe and effective. The district court held there is no such right. A divided panel of this Court held there is. Because we conclude that there is no fundamental right "deeply rooted in this Nation's history and tradition" of access to experimental drugs for the terminally ill (*Washington v. Glucksberg*), we affirm the judgment of the district court.

The Abigail Alliance for Better Access to Developmental Drugs (the "Alliance") is an organization of terminally ill patients and their supporters that seeks expanded access to experimental drugs for the terminally ill. The Food, Drug, and Cosmetic Act ("FDCA" or "Act"), however, generally prohibits access to new drugs unless and until they have been approved by the Food and Drug Administration ("FDA"). Gaining FDA approval can be a long process. First, an experimental drug's sponsor (*e.g.*, a drug company) must submit an application for approval. Because no drug may be approved without a finding of "substantial evidence that the drug will have the effect it purports or is represented to have," an application must contain "full reports of investigations which have been made to show whether or not such drug is safe for use and whether such drug is effective in use." Such reports rely in large measure on clinical trials with human subjects.

But before a sponsor can even begin human testing, it must submit for the FDA's approval an investigational new drug application, containing detailed information establishing that human testing is appropriate. Once the application for human testing has been approved, several phases of clinical testing begin. The Alliance's amended complaint alleges that this testing process is an extremely lengthy one, requiring nearly seven years for the average experimental drug. . . .

Terminally ill patients need not, however, always await the results of the clinical testing process. The FDA and Congress have created several programs designed to provide early access to promising experimental drugs when warranted. For example, under the "treatment IND" program, the FDA may approve use of an investigational drug by patients not part of the clinical trials for the treatment of "serious or immediately life-threatening disease[s]" if there exists "no comparable or satisfactory alternative drug or other therapy," if "[t]he drug is under investigation in a controlled clinical trial," and if the drug's sponsor "is actively pursuing marketing approval of the investigational drug with due diligence. . . ." Sponsors may not profit from any approved treatment IND program and may only "recover costs of manufacture, research, development, and handling of the investigational drug."

The Abigail Alliance's Proposals

Concluding that the FDA's current process for early access to new drugs was inadequate to meet the needs of its terminally ill members, the Alliance submitted its own proposals to the FDA. Those proposals culminated in a "citizen petition" to the FDA, arguing that there is a "different risk-benefit tradeoff facing patients who are terminally ill and who have no other treatment options. . . ." The Alliance's proposal suggested that the FDA allow early access based upon "the risk of illness, injury, or death from the disease in the absence of the drug.". . .

The FDA concluded that accepting the Alliance's proposal "would upset the appropriate balance that [it is] seeking to maintain, by giving almost total weight to the goal of early availability and giving little recognition to the importance of marketing drugs with reasonable knowledge for patients and physicians of their likely clinical benefit and their toxicity."

Having thus been rejected by the FDA, the Alliance turned to the courts, arguing that the United States Constitution provides a right of access to experimental drugs for its members. In a complaint that mirrored much of its earlier submissions to the FDA, the Alliance argued that the FDA's lengthy clinical trials, combined with the "FDA's restrictions on pre-approval availability[,] amount to a death sentence for these [terminally ill] patients. . . ."

As framed by the Alliance, we now consider: "Whether the liberty protected by the Due Process Clause embraces the right of a terminally ill patient with no remaining approved treatment options to decide, in consultation with his or her own doctor, whether to seek access to investigational medications that the [FDA] concedes are safe and promising enough for substantial human testing. . . ."

We do not address the broader question of whether access to medicine might ever implicate fundamental rights.

Constitutional Rights

The Due Process Clause of the Fifth Amendment provides that "[n]o person shall be . . . deprived of life, liberty, or property, without due process of law." The Supreme Court has held that the protections of the Amendment "guarantee more than fair process" (*Glucksberg*). The Court has stated that "[t]he Clause . . . provides heightened protection against government interference with certain fundamental rights and liberty interests," including "the rights to marry, to have children, to direct the education and upbringing of one's children, to marital privacy, to use contraception, to bodily integrity, and to abortion" (*Glucksberg*).

As such rights are not set forth in the language of the Constitution, the Supreme Court has cautioned against expanding the substantive rights protected by the Due Process Clause. . . . There is an additional and substantial concern that courts must also consider: "By extending constitutional protection to an asserted right or liberty interest, we, to a great extent, place, the matter outside the arena of public debate and legislative action." *Glucksberg*. Thus, the Supreme Court has directed courts to "exercise the utmost care whenever we are asked to break new ground in this field, lest the liberty protected by the Due Process Clause be subtly transformed into the policy preferences of the [courts' members]. . . ."

In *Glucksberg*, the Supreme Court described its "established method of substantive-due-process analysis" as having "two primary features."

> First, we have regularly observed that the Due Process Clause specially protects those fundamental rights and liberties which are, objectively, deeply rooted in this Nation's history and tradition and implicit in the concept of ordered liberty, such that neither liberty nor justice would exist if they were sacrificed. Second, we have required in substantive-due-process cases a careful description of the asserted fundamental liberty interest.

We will assume *arguendo* [for the sake of argument] that the Alliance's description of its asserted right would satisfy *Glucksberg*'s "careful description" requirement. Looking to whether the Alliance has demonstrated that its right is deeply rooted in this Nation's history, tradition, and practices, the Alliance's claim for constitutional protection rests on two arguments: (1) that "common law and historical American practices have traditionally trusted individual doctors and their patients with almost complete autonomy to evaluate the efficacy of medical treatments"; and (2) that FDA policy is "inconsistent with the way that our legal tradition treats persons in all other life-threatening situations." More specifically, the Alliance argues that the concepts of self-defense, necessity, and interference with rescue are broad enough to demonstrate the existence of the fundamental right they seek—a right for "persons in mortal peril" to "try to save their own lives, even if the chosen means would otherwise be illegal or involve enormous risks. . . ."

Effectiveness vs. Safety

The Alliance argues that its right can be found in our history and legal traditions because "the government never interfered with the judgment of individual doctors about the medical *efficacy* of particular drugs until 1962. . . ."

The Alliance has little to say, however, about our Nation's history of regulating the *safety* of drugs. The Alliance's effort to focus on efficacy regulation ignores one simple fact: it is unlawful for the Alliance to procure experimental drugs not only because they have not been proven effective, but because they have not been proven safe. . . .

Examining, as we are required to do under *Glucksberg*, our Nation's history, legal traditions, and practice with respect to the regulation of drugs for efficacy and safety, we conclude that our Nation has long expressed interest in drug regulation, calibrating its response in terms of the capabilities to determine the risks associated with both drug safety and efficacy. . . .

The Alliance argues that, prior to 1962, patients were free to make their own decisions whether a drug might be effective. But even assuming *arguendo* that efficacy regulation began in 1962, the Alliance's argument ignores our Nation's history of drug safety regulation. . . .

Even setting the safety issue to one side, the Alliance's argument that effectiveness was not required before 1962 also fails under closer scrutiny. First, as a matter of history, at least some drug regulation prior to 1962 addressed efficacy. More importantly, an arguably limited history of efficacy regulation prior to 1962 does not establish a fundamental right of access to unproven drugs. The amendments made to the FDCA by Congress throughout the twentieth century demonstrate that Congress and the FDA have continually responded to new risks presented by an evolving technology. Recent government efficacy regulation has reflected Congress's exercise of its well-established power to regulate in response to scientific, mathematical, and medical advances.

True, a lack of government interference throughout history might be some evidence that a right is deeply rooted. But standing alone, it cannot be enough. If it were, it would be easy to employ such a premise to support sweeping claims of fundamental rights. For example, one might argue that, because Congress did not significantly regulate marijuana until 1937, relatively late in the constitutional day, there must be a tradition of protecting marijuana use. Because Congress did not regulate narcotics until 1866 when it heavily taxed opium, a drug created long before our Nation's founding, it must be that individuals have a right to acquire and use narcotics free from regulation. Or because speed limits are a recent innovation, we have a fundamental right to drive as fast as we deem fit. . . . Indeed, creating constitutional rights to be free from regulation based solely upon a prior lack of regulation would undermine much of the modern administrative state, which, like drug regulation, has increased in scope as changing conditions have warranted.

Life-Threatening Situations

The Alliance next turns to several common law doctrines, arguing that barring access to experimental drugs for terminally ill patients is "inconsistent with the way that our legal tradition treats persons in all other life-threatening situations." Specifically, the Alliance argues that three doctrines—(1) the doctrine of necessity; (2) the tort [act for which someone can be sued] of intentional interference with rescue; and (3) the right to self-defense—each support the recognition of a right to self-preservation. Such a right to self-preservation, the Alliance believes, would permit "persons in mortal peril . . . to try to save their own lives, even if the chosen means would otherwise be illegal or involve enormous risks. . . ."

The Supreme Court's analysis of the common law doctrine of necessity in *United States v. Oakland Cannabis Buyers' Cooperative* leaves little room for the Alliance's argument that common law necessity could justify overriding the Food, Drug, and Cosmetic Act.

In *United States v. Oakland Cannabis Buyers' Cooperative*, a group of patients seeking access to marijuana for medicinal purposes argued that "because necessity was a defense at common law, medical necessity should be read into the Controlled Substances Act." The Supreme Court rejected that argument because "[u]nder any conception of legal necessity, one principle is clear: The defense cannot succeed when the legislature itself has made a determination of values. . . ."

The Alliance next invokes the tort of intentional interference with lifesaving efforts, which the Restatement of Torts defines as "intentionally prevent[ing] a third person from giving to another aid *necessary* to his bodily security." But that is not this case. The Alliance seeks access to drugs that are experimental and have not been shown to be safe, let alone effective at (or "necessary" for) prolonging life. Indeed, the Alliance concedes that taking experimental drugs can "involve enormous risks." In essence, the Alliance insists on a constitutional right to assume any level of risk. It is difficult to see how a tort addressing interference with providing "necessary" aid would guarantee a constitutional right to override the collective judgment of the scientific and medical communities expressed through the FDA's clinical testing process. Thus, we cannot agree that the tort of intentional interference with rescue evidences a right of access to experimental drugs.

Finally, the Alliance looks to traditional self-defense principles to support its proposed constitutional right. . . . So, the argument goes, if victims of crimes are allowed to assume these risks in defending their lives, terminally ill patients should also be allowed to assume the risk that an experimental drug may hasten their deaths.

That self-defense principles should be applied in the medical context is evidenced, the Alliance argues, by the Supreme Court's abortion jurisprudence [collection of decisions]. The Alliance does not look to the "right of personal privacy" addressed in *Roe v. Wade*. Instead, the Alliance argues that *Roe* "recognized another, entirely separate right to abortion: a woman's right to abort a fetus *at any stage of a pregnancy* if doing so is necessary to preserve her life or health." "That right," the Alliance argues, "is grounded in traditional self-defense principles rather than privacy. . . ." Applying that concept here, the Alliance argues that because its terminally ill members are in immediate danger of harm from cancer, they can use whatever medical means are necessary to defend themselves. Thus, they argue, even if a medical treatment might otherwise be prohibited by law, the doctrine of self-defense justifies access to that treatment, just as self-defense justifies an assault victim using physical force otherwise prohibited by law.

This analogy also fails because this case is not about using reasonable force to defend oneself (as in most cases involving self-defense), nor is it about access to life-saving medical treatment. This case is about whether there is a constitutional right to assume, in the Alliance's own words, "enormous risks," in pursuit of *potentially* life-saving drugs. Unlike the cases in which the doctrine of self-defense might properly be invoked, this case involves risk from drugs with no proven therapeutic effect, which at a minimum separates this example from the abortion "life of the mother" exception. Because terminally ill patients cannot fairly be characterized as using reasonable force to defend themselves when they take unproven and possibly unsafe drugs, the Alliance's desire that the terminally ill be free to assume the risk of experimental drugs cannot draw support from the doctrine of self-defense.

The Claimed Rights Is Not Fundamental

Although it has not addressed the precise constitutional argument urged by the Alliance, we find it highly significant that the Supreme Court has rejected several similar challenges to the FDCA and related laws brought on statutory ground. . . . And other courts have rejected arguments that the Constitution provides an affirmative right of access to particular medical treatments reasonably prohibited by the Government.

In keeping with those decisions, we conclude that the Alliance has not provided evidence of a right to procure and use experimental drugs that is deeply rooted in our Nation's history and traditions. To the contrary, our Nation's history evidences increasing regulation of drugs as both the ability of government to address these risks has increased and the risks associated with drugs have become apparent. Similarly, our legal traditions of allowing a necessity defense, prohibiting intentional interference with rescue, and recognizing a right of self-defense cannot justify creating a constitutional right to assume any level of risk without regard to the scientific and medical judgment expressed through the clinical testing process.

Because the Alliance's claimed right is not fundamental, the Alliance's claim of a right of access to experimental drugs is subject only to rational basis scrutiny. . . .

The Alliance acknowledges the risk inherent in taking experimental drugs. The Alliance would rather that individual patients make decisions about this risk than have the FDA decide which drugs are safe enough for limited access to the terminally ill. The FDA counters that "[w]ithout a requirement of FDA approval, patients could be exposed to unreasonable risks from investigational drugs that may be neither safe nor effective."

Applying the rational basis standard to the Alliance's complaint, we cannot say that the government's interest does not bear a rational relation to a legitimate state interest. That conclusion is compelled by the Supreme Court's decision in *United States v. Rutherford*. In that case, terminally ill patients sought to prevent the FDA from prohibiting access to the drug laetrile, even though the drug had not been approved for public use. In rejecting a challenge by terminally ill patients claiming that the FDCA's safety requirement did not apply to them, the

Supreme Court held that "[f]or the terminally ill, as for any-one else, a drug is unsafe if its potential for inflicting death or physical injury is not offset by the possibility of therapeutic benefit. . . ."

Although terminally ill patients desperately need curative treatments, as *Rutherford* holds, their deaths can certainly be hastened by the use of a potentially toxic drug with no proven therapeutic benefit. Thus, we must conclude that, prior to dis-tribution of a drug outside of controlled studies, the Govern-ment has a rational basis for ensuring that there is a scientifi-cally and medically acceptable level of knowledge about the risks and benefits of such a drug. We therefore hold that the FDA's policy of limiting access to investigational drugs is ra-tionally related to the legitimate state interest of protecting patients, including the terminally ill, from potentially unsafe drugs with unknown therapeutic effects.

Balance of Risks and Benefits Should Be Decided by Legislation

Although in the Alliance's view the FDA has unjustly erred on the side of safety in balancing the risks and benefits of experi-mental drugs, this is not to say that the FDA's balance can never be changed. The Alliance's arguments about morality, quality of life, and acceptable levels of medical risk are cer-tainly ones that can be aired in the democratic branches, without injecting the courts into unknown questions of sci-ence and medicine. Our Nation's history and traditions have consistently demonstrated that the democratic branches are better suited to decide the proper balance between the uncer-tain risks and benefits of medical technology, and are entitled to deference in doing so. As the Supreme Court has held [in *Jacobson v. Massachusetts*]

> We must assume that, when the statute in question was passed, the legislature . . . was not unaware of these oppos-ing theories, and was compelled, of necessity, to choose be-

tween them. It was not compelled to commit a matter involving the public health and safety to the final decision of a court or jury. It is no part of the function of a court or a jury to determine which one of two modes was likely to be the most effective for the protection of the public against disease. . . .

Consistent with that precedent, our holding today ensures that this debate among the Alliance, the FDA, the scientific and medical communities, and the public may continue through the democratic process.

> *"It is no more than tragic wordplay to suggest that the Alliance's liberty claim to potentially life-prolonging medications . . . does not involve a corollary to the right to life enshrined in the Fifth Amendment to the Constitution."*

Dissenting Opinion: Liberty to Use Potentially Lifesaving Medications Is Required by the Constitutionally Protected Right to Life

Judith Ann Wilson Rogers

Judith Ann Wilson Rogers has been a federal judge on the United States Court of Appeals for the District of Columbia Circuit since 1994. She was the first African American woman to become a circuit court judge. The following viewpoint is her dissent in the case of Abigail Alliance for Better Access to Developmental Drugs v. von Eschenbach, *in which the Court of Appeals ruled that terminally ill patients do not have a constitutional right to use experimental drugs that have not been approved by the FDA. In Judge Rogers' opinion, the court's decision was entirely wrong and was based on confusion of issues. It ignored the Constitution's emphasis on life, focusing instead on whether the government has a compelling interest in regulating drugs—which, she says, is secondary to the question of whether a fundamental right to protect one's own life exists. She declares*

Judith Ann Wilson Rogers, dissenting opinion, *Abigail Alliance for Better Access to Developmental Drugs v. Andrew von Eschenbach*, United States Court of Appeals for the District of Columbia Circuit, August 7, 2007. http://pacer.cadc.uscourts.gov/docs/common/opinions/200708/04-5350c.pdf

that it does, and that the court was misguided in claiming that a historical lack of interference with that right is not enough to show that it is deep-rooted. It is contrary to the Nation's tradition of liberty, she says, to deny patients their only chance to survive.

Today, the court rejects the claim that terminally ill patients who have exhausted all government-approved treatment options have a fundamental right to access investigational new drugs. The court's opinion reflects a flawed conception of the right claimed by the Abigail Alliance for Better Access to Developmental Drugs and a stunning misunderstanding of the stakes. The court shifts the inquiry required by *Washington v. Glucksberg*, by changing the nature of the right, by conflating the right with the deprivation, and by prematurely advancing countervailing government interests. The court fails to come to grips with the Nation's history and traditions, which reflect deep respect and protection for the right to preserve life, a corollary to the right to life enshrined in the Constitution. The court confuses this liberty interest with the manner in which the Alliance alleges that the liberty has been deprived, namely by denying terminally ill patients access to investigational medications under the narrow conditions described by the Alliance. The court conflates the inquiry as to whether a fundamental right exists at all with whether the government has demonstrated a compelling interest, when strictly scrutinized, rendering its restrictive policy constitutional.

These missteps lead the court to rely upon how rights and liberties have been limited and restricted—addressing regulations to prevent fraud in the sale of misbranded and adulterated medications or safety restrictions applicable to all medicines for any palliative purpose—which says little about the historic importance of the underlying right of a person to save her own life. Likewise, in its treatment of the common law doctrines of necessity, interference with rescue, and self defense, the court points to evolved limitations on those doctrines while ignoring the core concerns that animate them, namely the special importance of life and attempts to preserve it. That the ultimate protection of such varying attempts to save life is cabined by the precedents—regarding what constitutes "necessity," the related "necessity" of any aid being given to a third party, and the "reasonable" and "necessary" limitations on any force used in self-defense—does not suggest the absence of an underlying right to attempt to protect life, but rather the recognition of competing governmental interests that in various circumstances justify the deprivation of or a limitation upon the right.

The Right to Life Is Fundamental

The common law doctrines remain good evidence of a history and tradition of protecting life and attempts to preserve life as a deep-seated personal right. That the right may be and has been denied in the face of compelling governmental interests is no reason for conflating the two stages of the analysis and looking only to the results of past cases in order to avoid the analysis prescribed by the Supreme Court in *Glucksberg*, Contrary to today's view of the court and the Federal Drug Administration ("FDA"), nothing in the prior opinion of the court would give "total weight" to the interests of the terminal patients or deny the FDA the ability to put its competing governmental interests into the balance. The court was explicit on this point, requiring precisely such weighing and proof of the proposed government concerns, rather than merely accepting, under the rubric of rational basis scrutiny, any assertions the FDA chooses to offer.

In the end, it is startling that the oft-limited rights to marry, to fornicate, to have children, to control the education and upbringing of children, to perform varied sexual acts in private, and to control one's own body even if it results in one's own death or the death of a fetus have all been deemed fundamental rights covered, although not always protected, by the Due Process Clause, but the right to try to save one's life is left out in the cold despite its textual anchor in the right to life. This alone is reason the court should pause about refusing to put the FDA to its proof when it denies terminal patients with no alternative therapy the only option they have left, regardless of whether that option may be a long-shot with high risks. The court is on even weaker footing when it relies upon the risks entailed in medical procedures to wrest life-and-death decisions that once were vested in patients and their physicians. The court commits a logical error of dramatic consequence by concluding that the investigational drugs are somehow not "necessary." While the potential cures may not prove *sufficient* to save the life of a terminally ill patient, they are surely *necessary* if there is to be any possibility of preserving her life.

It bears outlining the history and common law basis for the Alliance's claim in order to demonstrate, once again, that the history and traditions of this Nation support the right of a terminal patient, and not the government, to make this fundamentally personal choice involving her own life. Because judicial precedents and the historical record require strict scrutiny before upsetting rights of this magnitude, the FDA must demonstrate a compelling governmental interest before its policy restricting access can survive. Accordingly, I would remand the case to the district court to make the initial determination as to whether FDA has met its burden, and I respectfully dissent. . . .

The court . . . makes the wholly unsupported assertion that "the collective judgment of the scientific and medical communities [is] expressed through the FDA's clinical testing process." To the contrary, the Alliance specifically alleges in attachments to its complaint that the FDA has denied terminally ill Alliance members access to investigational new drugs "reported to have great potential," and acknowledged by the "medical community" as "far and away ... superior to anything then available." Thus, there are situations where a terminally ill patient seeks access to a new medication that has not yet been approved by the FDA for commercial marketing but that has been recognized by the medical community as that patient's best chance to survive. In such instances, the Fifth Amendment guarantee of due process protects the terminally ill patient's pursuit of those medications.

There is, then, no merit to the FDA's suggestion adopted by the court that in the medical context there can be no deeply rooted privilege to attempt to save one's own life with medical advances because medical advances capable of saving lives are a relatively recent phenomenon. . . .

The Due Process Clause Protects Life and Liberty

Against [the] substantial historical record demonstrating the deep roots of the right to preserve one's own life, it is no coincidence that neither the court nor the FDA can marshal evidence from the early history of the Nation demonstrating that the federal government or any state thought to restrain the terminally ill from accessing medical treatments and procedures that had not proven unsafe but were of unknown efficacy. Still, the court asserts that "a lack of government interference ... cannot be enough" to demonstrate that a right is deeply rooted. This reasoning is misguided.

First, the most fundamental rights are those that no government of the people would contemplate abridging—it is doubtful that many courts or legislatures have discussed whether the government can determine whether we are allowed to breathe air, but this does not make our access to oxygen any less grounded in history. . . . In considering whether the terminally ill patient's interest in self-preservation is protected by the Due Process Clause, the court overlooks the most fundamental evidence of the protection that the Alliance claims, namely that the words "life" and "liberty" are in the Due Process Clause itself. The right to life, and the asserted corollary right to attempt to preserve life, is not a second derivative species of "liberty" whose protection by the Constitution should be approached with skepticism. Insofar as courts should be skeptical of interfering with the legislative debate and ongoing democratic discussions about fundamental issues of life and death, that skepticism is better applied to the latter portion of the strict scrutiny analysis—the evaluation of the competing government interests and the greater or lesser narrowness of the tailoring required in the face of scientific uncertainty and conflicting opinions. To deny the constitutional importance of the right to life and to attempt to preserve life is to move from judicial modesty to judicial abdication, as well as confusion, and deprive an express constitutional interest of its due weight in the court's analysis.

Second, the Supreme Court's statements on fundamental rights do not support the court's conclusion. . . .

Third, the court's concern that "such a premise [would] support sweeping claims of fundamental rights" neglects the existence of the second *Glucksberg* criterion. Strict scrutiny is not triggered just by a history of protection—otherwise, the entire common law would be constitutionalized. It is the second requirement, that a right be "'implicit in the concept of ordered liberty,' such that 'neither liberty nor justice would exist if they were sacrificed,'" that guards against unwarranted expansion of substantive due process rights. Just as in the context of the necessity defense at common law, the court conflates these two distinct inquiries, and in its haste to acquire a limiting principle, it constructs a significant and unwarranted roadblock to judicial recognition of fundamental rights. . . .

Fourth, in the alternative, the court shifts the target and looks to historical evidence of regulation for *safety*. The court claims that post-Phase I testing is designed not only to test a drug's efficacy but also to continue monitoring its safety. As support, the court lists instances in which drugs have been removed from the market after Phase I because of safety concerns. This inquiry confuses the right—to save one's life—with the alleged deprivation, which here occurs by means of an agency policy. Whether the FDA policy actually impermissibly infringes upon the asserted right is a factual question that is not properly resolved at the motion-to-dismiss stage when all reasonable inferences must be drawn to the plaintiff's benefit. Furthermore, safety restrictions are applicable to all medicines for any pallative purpose, as well as illegal drugs that serve no pallative purpose, and therefore tell us little about the regulation of potentially life-saving medicines sought by terminally ill patients who have no alternative treatment options. . . .

Regulation of Drugs Is Recent

For more than half of this Nation's history, . . . until the enactment of the 1906 Act, a person could obtain access to any new drug without any government interference whatsoever. Even after enactment of the FDCA in 1938, Congress imposed no limitation on the commercial marketing of new drugs based upon the drugs' efficacy. Rather, at that time, the FDA could interrupt the sale of new drugs only if it determined that the new drug was unsafe. Government regulation of such drugs premised on concern over a new drug's efficacy, as opposed to its safety, is of very recent origin. Even today, a patient may use a drug for unapproved purposes where the drug may be unsafe or ineffective for the off-label purpose. In short, encumbrances on the treatment decisions of a patient and her physician lack the historical pedigree of the rights that the Alliance seeks to vindicate.

Instead of confronting this history, the court relies on statutory restrictions that address misbranded or adulterated drugs, sales of poisons, and fraudulent curative claims, government restrictions that are not inconsistent with the right of a person to attempt to save her own life. None of the cited restrictions, focusing largely on the licensing of pharmacists, suggest a physician could not prescribe a new medication for a terminal patient. While Congress has imposed increased responsibilities on the drug industry and the FDA upon evidence of tragic consequences of some new drugs as a result of new technology, the FDA does not regulate physicians, and off-label prescription of medications is a long-standing practice that has not been outlawed. Elsewhere the court relies on straw men that are either acknowledged by the court to be irrelevant, or are in fact irrelevant, or are speculative. This analysis hardly overcomes the history and Constitutional recognition of the underlying right to life that the Alliance claims.

The common law traditions protecting necessity, forbidding interference with rescue, and supporting self-defense, and the Supreme Court's validation of the fundamental right of a pregnant woman to undergo a medical procedure to save her own life demonstrate that the protected liberty interest of the terminally ill to choose whether to pursue prescription medications that may save their lives is deeply rooted in this Nation's history. Nothing in the history of drug regulation demonstrates otherwise. . . .

Autonomy Is the Core of Liberty

Setting aside the textual anchor of the Alliance's claim in the right to life, the claimed right also falls squarely within the realm of rights implicit in ordered liberty. The core of liberty is autonomy. As Professor Charles Fried writes, "[l]iberty is the exercise of our powers as self-conscious, judging individuals, individuals who in making our own lives cannot be responsible to anyone . . . else except as we choose to be." It is difficult to imagine any context in which this liberty interest would be stronger than in trying to save one's own life.

The Supreme Court engaged in similar analysis in *Cruzan*. In evaluating the claim that due process protects a person's right to refuse life-sustaining treatment, the Court reasoned that "it cannot be disputed that the Due Process Clause protects an interest in life as well as an interest in refusing life-sustaining medical treatment." The Court acknowledged that "[t]he principle that a competent person has a constitutionally protected liberty interest in refusing unwanted medical treatment," could be inferred from its prior decisions. Like the right claimed in *Cruzan*, the right claimed by the Alliance to be free of FDA imposition does not involve treatment by the government or a government subsidy. Rather, the Alliance seeks only to have the government step aside so as not to interfere with the individual right of self-determination. . . .

For these reasons, I have serious disagreements with the court's assessment of the Alliance's claim to a fundamental right protected by the Fifth Amendment to the Constitution. It is no more than tragic wordplay to suggest that the Alliance's liberty claim to potentially life-prolonging medications, when no other government approved alternatives exist, does not involve a corollary to the right to life enshrined in the Fifth Amendment to the Constitution. Denying a terminally ill patient her only chance to survive without even a strict showing of governmental necessity presupposes a dangerous brand of paternalism. As the court phrases it, because "*[w]e* . . . cannot know until the clinical testing process has been completed that these drugs are necessary," the terminally ill patient, informed by her physician, is denied a right to decide whether to bear those risks in an attempt to preserve her life. Such intervention is directly at odds with this Nation's history and traditions giving recognition to individual self-determination and autonomy where one's own life is at stake and should extend no further than the result in this case. Because the right of a terminally ill patient to access potentially life-saving investigational medications satisfies the *Glucksberg* test, I would remand this case for the district court to assess in the first instance whether there exists a compelling governmental interest, narrowly tailored, to overcome the Alliance's interest.

"The FDA, for all its shortcomings, is the main barrier that exists against the domination of the [drug] market by hype."

Allowing Terminally Ill Patients to Use Unproven Drugs Would Hinder the Clinical Trial Process

Ralph W. Moss

Ralph W. Moss is a medical writer specializing in cancer treatments. In the following viewpoint, which was written after a small panel of Circuit Court judges ruled in favor of allowing terminally ill patients to use unapproved drugs but before the full court reversed that decision, he declares that premature use of such drugs would be a dangerous mistake. Most new anticancer drugs do not save lives, he says; even those that shrink tumors generally extend life by only a few months. Patients have a false impression of what they can gain from them, which is encouraged by the drug companies. Few will agree to enter randomized clinical trials if the new drugs being tested are already obtainable. In Moss's opinion, making such drugs available would not be in the best interests of cancer patients because it would make it more difficult to find out which actually work.

Last month [May 2006], the U.S. Court of Appeals for the District of Columbia made a decision of huge consequence. It ruled that terminally ill cancer patients have a constitutional right to treatments that have not yet been approved

Ralph W. Moss, "No Way to Save a Life," *New Scientist Magazine*, June 3, 2006. Reproduced by permission.

by the Food and Drug Administration (FDA). As long as such drugs have completed phase I clinical trials, the court stated, they should be made available to any patient who requests them.

The three-judge panel split 2–1 in favour of a suit brought by the Abigail Alliance for Better Access to Developmental Drugs, a patient advocacy group that has been lobbying hard to bring new medicines to terminally ill patients. The decision is ominous because it is likely to undermine the drug evaluation process, which has been under attack for over a decade. In another worrying development, last November [2005] Republican senator Sam Brownback introduced a bill into the Senate aimed at accelerating the approval system for drugs, biological products and medical devices. It would give patients access to treatments that have shown promise but have not been proven. If enacted, this bill could lead to an anarchic jumble of ineffective and potentially unsafe treatments on the market.

The *Abigail* case and the Congressional initiative are part of a widespread effort to reduce the requirement that new drugs go through extensive and rigorous testing before being sold to the public. The FDA, and the Bush administration that it serves, have ostensibly opposed Abigail's efforts. For example, the FDA argued that it already had plans to make potentially lifesaving drugs available before the completion of the lengthy three-phase clinical trial process. It also claimed that allowing large numbers of patients to receive unapproved drugs could put many of them at unacceptable risk, even if they were terminally ill. But the FDA's opposition was undercut by its own increasing reliance on the so-called accelerated approval programme, under which drugs are often approved before there is proof of clinical benefit.

Effectiveness of New Drugs Is Overestimated

One drug approved in this way was Iressa, a treatment for advanced lung cancer, which was given the green light by the

FDA on the basis of questionable phase II trial results, ignoring compelling phase III trials showing that the drug was ineffective and more toxic than anticipated. So the drug approval process had already begun to fray at the edges before the Appeals court judges made their ruling last month. Their decision could accelerate that trend: the judges ruled that the FDA's normal regulatory activity interfered with efforts that could save a terminally ill patient's life.

While that sentiment is seemingly humane, it is based on a false premise, for it wildly overestimates the effectiveness of most new anti-cancer drugs. It ignores the fact that there are very few truly lifesaving drugs for the advanced stages of any kind of adult cancer. Most new "targeted" drugs, when combined with conventional chemotherapy, extend life by a few months at best. Yet these drugs are widely perceived as a revolutionary new departure in cancer treatment—an impression that drug companies have done little to dispel.

The vast majority of drugs in phase I trials are not lifesaving; they are not even life-prolonging. More crucially, it is only through the successful completion of arduous phase II and phase III trials that drugs can ever be proven to be beneficial. By allowing the drug approval process to be truncated, as the judges propose, the potential for gathering important information on the safety, toxicity and effectiveness of new treatments is severely curtailed. This spells doom for the randomised clinical trial process. Few patients are likely to agree to enter phase II or III trials with the same agent that will be freely available after small phase I studies. Most likely, cancer patients will increasingly fall prey to exaggerated claims for various half-baked drugs, as a result of skilful manipulation of public opinion through publicity.

Premature Availability Will Make It Harder to Find Out Which Drugs Work

At the end of phase I trials, scientists, industry officials, regulators and the public still know next to nothing about the drug in question, least of all its effectiveness. The purpose of phase I is simply to evaluate a drug's safety, determine a workable dosage range and identify side effects. Granted, some clinical effects such as tumour shrinkages may be seen in a few patients, but this is incidental information—and the temporary shrinkage of a tumour seldom correlates with a prolongation of life.

Much of the information that patients receive about new drugs is of a dubious kind. The FDA, for all its shortcomings, is the main barrier that exists against the domination of the market by hype. But since the Clinton years, and especially during the George Bush era, the FDA's vigilance over the cancer drug marketplace has been steadily eroded. The repercussions of this latest judicial decision are potentially disastrous. If it is allowed to stand, it will make the task of determining which drugs actually work much more difficult. That is hardly in the interest of cancer patients.

"If there is no requirement or incentive to continue costly research, pharmaceutical companies will allow potentially unsafe and ineffective experimental drugs to flood the market."

Giving Terminally Ill Patients Access to Unapproved Drugs Would Lead to Marketing of Harmful Ones

Shira Bender, Lauren Flicker, and Rosamond Rhodes

Rosamond Rhodes is a professor of medical education and director of bioethics education at the Mount Sinai School of Medicine and a professor of philosophy at the Graduate Center, City University of New York. At the time the following article was written, Shira Bender and Lauren Flicker, both students at the University of Pennsylvania, were her summer interns. In this viewpoint, written before the final ruling in Abigail v. Eschenbach, *they point out that helping people who are terminally ill is not the only thing at stake. In the authors' opinion, the probable harm to others—the effect that allowing patients access to experimental drugs would have on society, science, and medicine—should also be considered. People who believed they had been helped by an unproven drug could create a public demand for it to be covered by insurance and widely adopted as a treatment, whether it actually worked or not. Those who had taken it would have to be excluded from clinical trials, so there might not be*

Shira Bender, Lauren Flicker, and Rosamond Rhodes, "Access for the Terminally Ill to Experimental Medical Innovations: A Three-Pronged Threat," *American Journal of Bioethics*, October 2007. Reproduced by permission of Taylor & Francis Group, LLC, http://www.informaworld.com, conveyed through Copyright Clearance Center, Inc.

enough patients left on whom it could be tested. Pharmaceutical companies would be unwilling to pay for expensive trials if their new drugs could be used without them, which means that the market would be flooded with potentially unsafe and ineffective drugs. Therefore, the authors say, premature use of such drugs should not be permitted even for the sake of preserving individual liberty.

Dr. Arthur Caplan's recent editorial in the *American Journal of Bioethics* draws attention to the significant issue of whether to allow the terminally ill access to experimental medical innovations. He responds to the case of *Abigail Alliance for Better Access to Developmental Drugs v. Von Eschenbach*, which discusses the rights and liberties of individual terminally ill patients. The Plaintiff, the Abigail Alliance for Better Access to Developmental Drugs, advocates for access to experimental drugs for patients in dire need. In their suit, the Plaintiff argues that access to Phase I [experimental] drugs for terminally ill patients is a substantive due process right under the Fifth Amendment. They state in their proposed bill to amend the Federal Food Drug and Cosmetic Act: "Seriously ill patients have a right to access available investigational drugs, biological products, and devices." While he is sympathetic to the plight of terminally ill patients, Dr. Caplan's position is that the individual benefit of taking Phase I drugs is questionable, and that the Abigail Alliance lawsuit will not necessarily help them. We agree that helping patients in need and securing their rights are significant causes, and we feel that Dr. Caplan's response is compassionate and pertinent to the lawsuit. Nonetheless, both he and the majority opinion in *Abigail Alliance* have focused on the needs and rights of individual patients without addressing the potential risks to research that access to Phase I drugs could create.

It is our position that any discussion involving either a purported right to drug access or human subject research must address both the cost to the individual patient, as well as risks and harms that could be born by others. According to John Stuart Mill's Harm Principle, liberties may only be restricted in order to prevent harm to others. While the Court and Dr. Caplan focus primarily on the rights, safety and psychology of the individual terminally ill patient, they ignore the probable harmful effects that allowing patients access to Phase I drugs would have on society, science and medicine.

We identify three probable harms to others that allowing patients access to Phase I drugs would likely generate. We will discuss each of these harms in turn.

The Hype

Dr. Caplan writes about a well-known and largely unavoidable risk in research: the therapeutic misconception. In research, this means that subjects may falsely believe that they will receive therapeutic benefit from their participation in a study. Even after a subject is told that he or she may only receive a placebo, and that the drug being tested is not yet considered treatment, the expectation of benefit remains. The therapeutic misconception can be expected to arise when a patient uses a Phase I drug as treatment.

While Dr. Caplan focuses on the psychological risk of the therapeutic misconception to the patient, many others are also vulnerable to its affects. Once a patient or a group of patients uses experimental drugs, the beliefs generated will have consequences that extend far beyond the health of those individuals. For instance, imagine a patient with a terminal form of cancer who takes an experimental drug and a week later "miraculously" no longer shows symptoms. Whether he intends to or not, it is likely that he will attribute his recovery to the drug, as will his family, and eventually the media, and then the rest of society. This hype over the presumed effects of the drug could eventually reach other patients who are desperate for treatment, and could then snowball into public outcry and litigation, eventually forcing insurance companies to cover the cost of the drug as treatment and then to raise their premiums. Clinicians may also be influenced by the hype over the assumed effects of the drug, and then prescribe it to their patients. Consequently, researchers may have difficulty objectively conducting studies to discover whether or not the drug is effective. Rather, they may study the drug in the interest of confirming their and society's pre-existing belief in its effectiveness. . . .

The Human Resource

In research involving groups or populations of people with a particular illness or disease, each subject is a valuable resource. Furthermore, the greater the number of subjects included in a study, the more valuable the results will be, as their higher statistical significance will increase confidence in the conclusions they suggest. If some patients were allowed to use Phase I drugs as treatments, they would be excluded from participation in ongoing clinical studies of these drugs. For instance, if, after hearing the hype and exaggerated promise of an experimental drug, patients with a specific rare and terminal form of cancer were allowed to use it as treatment, there may not be enough people with that form of the disease on which to test the drugs. With an inadequate number of subjects to study, results would be delayed, and, in the most extreme cases, no evidence of efficacy could be supplied. . . .

To allow certain patients access to experimental drugs would deprive the general population of essential scientific and medical knowledge that could eventually lead to actual proven treatments, rather than to marketing products that have not been proven effective.

The Market

In 1938, Congress passed the Federal Food Drug and Cosmetic Act (FDCA), which required new drugs to be proven safe and effective before going to market, and started a new system of drug regulation. While only the Food and Drug Administration (FDA) holds the power to approve a drug, the FDCA placed the responsibility of safety and efficacy testing on pharmaceutical companies. Thus, in the interest of securing a profit, drug companies spend time, money and resources on creating and overseeing drug trials. . . . Clinical trials are costly, but pharmaceutical companies are aware that under the current regulation they cannot make a profit without the mandated testing. If the companies could make a profit without extensive testing, it would be hard to justify their continued funding of trials. Allowing terminally ill patients to use Phase I drugs would, therefore, provide incentive for pharmaceutical companies to bypass regulatory safeguards and costly requirements for collecting scientific proof of safety and efficacy.

The majority opinion in *Abigail Alliance* held that there was a substantive due process right for the terminally ill to have access to potentially life saving Phase I drugs, but it did not consider the social, political and economic consequences of such a holding. The dissenting judge, however, acknowledges these consequences. . . .

As the motivation to make experimental drugs available for treatment increases, the incentive and requirement to continue testing those drugs decreases. If there is no requirement or incentive to continue costly research, pharmaceutical companies will allow potentially unsafe and ineffective experimental drugs to flood the market.

Furthermore, the threat of litigation that patients currently hold over pharmaceutical companies would become obsolete if manufacturers were no longer liable for the safety and efficacy of their products. Without the incentive of avoiding lawsuits and minimizing liability through careful compliance with FDA drug testing polices, drug companies will have little need to uphold the reasonable degree of caution that current regulations mandate. Conversely, if courts were to hold that pharmaceutical companies were liable for any harm caused to patients using Phase I drugs, this would result in a flood of time-consuming and costly litigation. In the end, either drug companies will no longer be held accountable for marketing harmful experimental drugs, or there will be an excess of litigation, which would overwhelm the courts and possibly bankrupt pharmaceutical companies. In other words, eroding the current regulative control over drug development is likely to leave us all in harm's way. . . .

Phase I drugs are not treatments and should not be treated as such. To allow them to be used as treatments could hinder the scientific process, thus prolonging the suffering of thousands of patients who are waiting for researchers to find effective cures for their ailments. While we understand the emotional and psychological desire to help those in need, without study there is no way to know whether any intervention is harmful, beneficial or completely ineffective. The desire to help others should not be granted priority over sound scientific inquiry and proof. . . .

Compromising the drug development process, even in the interest of preserving individual liberty, is unacceptable because it can be expected to cause harm to others. . . .

Aside from the sort of limited and constrained exceptions already allowed, patients should not be given access to experimental drugs outside of controlled studies because hindering research would harm thousands of patients awaiting scientifically proven treatments.

"The Framers [of the Constitution]
would be appalled to see federal bureaucrats standing between dying patients and the medicines that might
save them."

The Constitution Was Written to Protect Liberty, Not Federal Regulatory Schemes

Roger Pilon

Roger Pilon is vice president for legal affairs at the Cato Institute and director of Cato's Center for Constitutional Studies. In the following viewpoint, he strongly criticizes the Circuit Court's ruling in Abigail Alliance for Better Access to Developmental Drugs v. von Eschenbach *on the grounds that it is contrary to the intent of the Constitution, which is to protect liberty. The decision shifted the burden of proof, Pilon says, from the government—which should have to justify restrictions on liberty—to dying patients, who cannot win as long as the government offers any reason at all for its regulations. He explains that this happened because many modern judges reverse the basic principle of the Constitution's Framers, who considered individual liberty more important than majority rule. The court in* Abigail *said the issue of access to drugs should be decided by the legislature— that is, by the majority—when in Pilon's opinion, its duty was to protect individuals against unrestrained government power.*

Roger Pilon, "The New Right to Life," *The Wall Street Journal*, August 10, 2007.
Copyright © 2007 Dow Jones & Company. All rights reserved. Reprinted with permission of *The Wall Street Journal* and the author.

T he wheels of justice turn slowly, especially for the dying. On Tuesday the D.C. Circuit, sitting *en banc* [in full court], reversed a 15-month-old decision by a panel of the court that had recognized a constitutional right of terminally ill patients to access potentially life-saving drugs not yet finally approved by the Food and Drug Administration. Given the poor quality of Tuesday's opinion in *Abigail Alliance for Better Access to Developmental Drugs v. Eschenbach*—"starting," said the dissent—one wonders why it took so long. The opinion's one virtue is that it brings out clearly how far modern "constitutional law" has strayed from the Constitution, a document written to protect liberty, not federal regulatory schemes.

The Right to Save One's Life Is Fundamental

Represented by the Washington Legal Foundation, Abigail Alliance is named for Abigail Burroughs, a 21-year-old college student who died of cancer in 2001. Their argument could not be more simple or straightforward, nor could Tuesday's dissent, written by Judge Judith Rogers and joined by Chief Judge Douglas Ginsburg, the majority in the earlier opinion. Citing the Fifth Amendment's right to life, the Ninth Amendment's assurance to the Constitution's ratifiers that the rights retained by the people far exceed those named in the document, and the Supreme Court's "fundamental rights" jurisprudence, Judge Rogers argued that the right to life, the right to self-preservation, and the right against interference with those rights—which the FDA is guilty of—are of one piece. They are deeply rooted in common law and the nation's history and traditions, implicit in the concept of ordered liberty, and thus "fundamental."

Indeed, it is startling, she noted, that the rights "to marry, to fornicate, to have children, to control the education and upbringing of children, to perform varied sexual acts in private, and to control one's own body have all been deemed fundamental, but the right to try to save one's life is left out in the cold despite its textual anchor in the right to life." Because the rights at issue here are "fundamental," she concluded, the court must apply, in judicial parlance, "strict scrutiny." The burden is on the FDA to show why its interference is justified—to show that its regulatory interests are compelling and its means narrowly tailored to serve those interests.

There, precisely, is where Tuesday's majority demurred. In a long footnote, Judge Thomas Griffith, who had dissented in the earlier opinion but wrote now for the majority, recast the right at issue as "the right to access experimental and unproven drugs in an attempt to save one's life." Through such "tragic wordplay," as the dissent put it, the right ceases to be "fundamental," under Supreme Court precedents, because it is "not deeply rooted in the Nation's history and traditions."

So described, the right is *not* "deeply rooted," of course, because the very idea of "experimental and unproven drugs" implies a regulatory regime like the FDA, and that is a recent development. Yet as the dissent detailed, for most of our history individuals were free to take whatever drugs they wanted without a doctor's prescription. It was only in 1951 that Congress created a category of *prescription* drugs. Then in 1962 it began requiring drug companies to conduct extensive tests to ensure drug "efficacy," which led to long delays for drug approval and to the deaths of countless patients who would gladly have borne the unknown risks for a chance at life.

As a legal matter, what Judge Griffith achieved with his linguistic legerdemain was a shift in the burden of proof: No longer would the government need to justify its restrictions; the dying would have to try to overcome those restrictions. But that would be impossible because now the court would no longer strictly scrutinize the government's rationale. Rather, it would apply a "rational basis" test under which the government would win as long as it had *any* reason for restricting access. Deference so complete, the dissent noted, amounts to nothing less than "judicial abdication."

The Issues Go Beyond This Case

Plainly, the issues here go well beyond this case, which is doubtless why the court decided to rehear it *en banc*. And they go beyond liberal and conservative as well, as the mixed seven who joined Judge Griffith's opinion should indicate. What we have here, arguably, is a revolt of sorts by Judge Rogers and Chief Judge Ginsburg against what passes today for "constitutional law." Reducing that revolt to a simple question: Under a Constitution that expressly protects the right to life, how did we get to where government can effectively restrict the right, and the courts will do nothing?

The answer for liberal jurists is simple. Since the Progressive Era they've worked assiduously to create the modern redistributive and regulatory state, constitutional impediments notwithstanding. Following Franklin Roosevelt's infamous 1937 threat to pack the Supreme Court with six new members, the Court facilitated that agenda by distinguishing "fundamental" and "nonfundamental" rights, protected by "strict scrutiny" and "rational basis scrutiny" respectively. That invention opened the floodgates to ever-expanding legislative schemes. But liberals didn't always win in the legislatures, so they turned increasingly to the courts, urging judges to find "fundamental" rights by consulting "evolving social values."

That led to a conservative backlash and a call for "judicial restraint," especially after the Court found a fundamental "right" to abortion in 1973. Both sides, therefore, have reasons to urge judicial restraint and deference to the administrative state. Modern liberals don't want judges interfering with the legislative creation of the welfare state's social and economic rights. Conservatives hope to frustrate those legislative efforts while forestalling the *judicial* creation of such rights. Thus, they urge judges to protect only those rights found expressly in the Constitution—and will describe rights, as here, to avoid even the hint of judicial activism.

In a word, then, liberal jurists could rule against Abigail Alliance to ensure the dominance of the regulatory regime.

Conservative jurists, viewing that regime as "settled law," could do likewise to avoid even the appearance of judicial activism. The approach of liberals is understandable: Long ago they abandoned the written for the "living" Constitution, which enables ad hoc adjudication, the rule of law notwithstanding. The approach of conservative "originalists," however, is less easily explained, since they purport to take the Constitution seriously.

Yet in Robert Bork's *The Tempting of America*, where conservatives often turn, we find an answer. Describing what he calls the "Madisonian dilemma," Judge Bork writes that America's "first principle is self-government, which means that in *wide areas* of life majorities are entitled to rule, if they wish, simply because they are majorities. The second principle is that there are nonetheless *some* things majorities must not do to minorities, *some* areas of life in which the individual must be free of majority rule." (emphasis added)

Individual Liberty Should Come First

That turns Madison on his head. James Madison stood for limited government, not wide-ranging democracy. His first principle was that in *wide areas* individuals are entitled to be free simply because they are born free. His second principle was that in *some* areas majorities are entitled to rule because we have authorized them to. That gets the order right: individual liberty first, self-government second, as a means for securing liberty.

Yet we repeatedly see conservative jurists, as here, ignoring the true Madison—deferring to the legislature when their duty, as Madison put it, is to stand as "an impenetrable bulwark against every assumption of power in the legislative or executive." A perfect example is Justice Antonin Scalia's dissent in a 2000 case, *Troxel v. Granville*, which found that Washington State's grandparent visitation act violated the right of fit parents to control access to their children. Dissenting, Justice Scalia argued that although the parental right is among the unalienable rights proclaimed by the Declaration of Independence and the unenumerated rights retained pursuant to the Ninth Amendment, that amendment does not authorize "judges to identify what [those rights] might be, and to enforce the judges' list against laws duly enacted by the people." Thus, just as the *Abigail Alliance* majority did, he would defer to the legislature to tell us what those rights are—the very legislature that had extinguished the parental right that he had just located in the Ninth Amendment.

The problem with that view, of course, is that it renders the Ninth Amendment a nullity—hardly what an originalist wants. Moreover, while recognizing retained unenumerated rights as "constitutional," it reduces them to a second class status since they are unenforceable. And that means they are not rights at all since rights are invoked, in the political context, only defensively, against threats from the majority. Yet on this view they can be extinguished by a mere majority.

There is, of course, no bright line between enumerated and unenumerated rights. In interpreting the Constitution, inferences are essential. As Judge Rogers put it, "were it impermissible to draw any inferences from a broader right to a narrower right, nearly all of the Supreme Court's substantive due process case law would be out of bounds." The only question, therefore, is whether the inferences are drawn correctly, and from sound underlying principles. To do that well, however, judges must have a sure grasp of those principles. That is the main problem today, as Tuesday's decision illustrates. The Framers would be appalled to see federal bureaucrats standing between dying patients and the medicines that might save them—sanctioned by a Constitution turned upside-down. Fortunately, this case will be appealed and the Supreme Court may yet examine it afresh.

Organizations to Contact

The editors have compiled the following list of organizations concerned with the issues debated in this book. The descriptions are derived from materials provided by the organizations. All have publications or information available for interested readers. The list was compiled on the date of publication of the present volume; the information provided here may change. Be aware that many organizations take several weeks or longer to respond to inquiries, so allow as much time as possible.

Abigail Alliance for Better Access to Developmental Drugs
36 Aspen Hill Dr., Fredericksburg, VA   22406
(540) 899-3766
E-mail: frankburroughs@abigail-alliance.org
Web site: www.abigail-alliance.org

This organization was founded by the father of Abigail Burroughs and was the petitioner in *Abigail Alliance for Better Access to Developmental Drugs v. Andrew von Eschenbach*. Its Web site contains detailed information about the case. The mission of the alliance is to educate the public on the need to have more expanded access and compassionate use programs for developmental cancer drugs and other developmental drugs for cancer patients and others who have run out of conventional treatment options, to work toward legislation that could help increase access to these drugs, and to help patients enter clinical trials.

Association of American Physicians and Surgeons (AAPS)
1601 N. Tucson Blvd., Ste. 9, Tucson, AZ   85716
(800) 635-1196 • Fax: (520) 325-4230
E-mail: aaps@aapsonline.org
Web site: www.aapsonline.org

The Association of American Physicians and Surgeons (AAPS) is a nonpartisan professional association of physicians dedicated to preserving the sanctity of the patient-physician relationship and the practice of private medicine. It supports the right of patients to free choice in medical care and opposes government involvement in medicine. It filed an amicus curiae (friend of the court) brief in *Sell v. United States*, which can be found at www.aapsonline.org/judicial/sell.htm, along with additional information about that case.

Center for Cognitive Liberty & Ethics (CCLE)
PO Box 73481, Davis, CA   95617
Fax: (205) 449-3119
Web site: http://cognitiveliberty.org

The Center for Cognitive Liberty & Ethics (CCLE) is a network of scholars aiming to develop social policies that will preserve and enhance freedom of thought into the twenty-first century, focusing especially on the effect of drugs on freedom of thought. It filed an amicus curiae (friend of the court) brief in *Sell v. United States*, which can be found at its Web site, along with additional information about that case.

Growth House
2215-R Market St. #199, San Francisco, CA   94114
(415) 863-3045
E-mail: info@growthhouse.org
Web site: www.growthhouse.org

Growth House is a gateway to resources for life-threatening illness and end-of-life care. Its primary mission is to improve the quality of compassionate care for people who are dying through public education and global professional collaboration. The Web site has extensive information on end-of-life subjects and links to other sites, including blogs, where these subjects are discussed. It also offers online discussion lists for health care professionals.

Hastings Center
21 Malcolm Gordon Rd., Garrison, NY   10524-4125
(845) 424-4040 • Fax: (845) 424-4545
E-mail: mail@thehastingscenter.org
Web site: www.thehastingscenter.org

The Hastings Center is an independent, nonpartisan, and nonprofit bioethics research institute that addresses fundamental and emerging questions in health care, biotechnology, and the environment, including those concerning end-of-life issues. It publishes a bimonthly journal, *The Hastings Report*, and many other reports and essays, some of which can be viewed on its Web site.

Institute for Health Freedom (IHF)
875 Eye St. NW, Ste. 500, Washington, DC   20006
(202) 429-6610 • Fax: (202) 861-1973
E-mail: feedback@ForHealthFreedom.org
Web site: www.ForHealthFreedom.org

The Institute for Health Freedom (IHF) is a nonpartisan, nonprofit research center that works to bring the issues of personal health freedom to the forefront of America's health policy debate. Its mission is to present the ethical and economic case for strengthening personal health freedom, defined as the freedom to choose one's health care providers and treatments, and to maintain confidential relationships with one's providers, without interference from government or private third parties. Its Web site contains material about issues related to informed consent, as well as other medical rights.

National Vaccine Information Center (NVIC)
204 Mill St., Ste. B1, Vienna, VA   22180
(703) 938-0342 • Fax: (703) 938-5768
Web site: www.nvic.org

The National Vaccine Information Center (NVIC), a national, nonprofit educational organization, is the oldest and largest consumer organization advocating the institution of vaccine safety and informed consent protections in the mass vaccination system. It is dedicated to the prevention of vaccine injuries and deaths through public education. As an independent clearinghouse for information on diseases and vaccines, NVIC does not promote the use of vaccines and does not advise against the use of vaccines; it supports the availability of all preventive health care options and the right of consumers to make educated, voluntary health care choices.

Society for Clinical Trials (SCT)
600 Wyndhurst Ave., Ste. 112, Baltimore, MD   21210
(410) 433-4722 • Fax: (410) 435-8631
E-mail: sctbalt@aol.com
Web site: www.sctweb.org

The Society for Clinical Trials (SCT) is an international professional organization dedicated to the development and dissemination of knowledge about the design, conduct, and analysis of government and industry-sponsored clinical trials and related health care research methodologies. It opposes giving terminally ill patients access to experimental drugs.

U.S. Food and Drug Administration Center for Drug Evaluation and Research (CDER)
5600 Fishers Ln., HFD-240, Rockville, MD   20857
(888) 463-6332
E-mail: druginfo@fda.hhs.gov
Web site: www.fda.gov/cder

The Center for Drug Evaluation and Research (CDER) is the U.S. government agency responsible for the testing of drugs. Its Web site offers detailed information about its policies and about specific drugs, including official consumer information sheets.

For Further Research

Books

George J. Annas, *American Bioethics: Crossing Human Rights and Health Law Boundaries.* New York: Oxford University Press, 2004.

————, *Judging Medicine.* Clifton, NJ: Humana Press, 1990.

————, *The Rights of Patients: The Authoritative ACLU Guide to the Rights of Patients.* New York: New York University Press, 2004.

William H. Colby, *Long Goodbye: The Deaths of Nancy Cruzan.* Carlsbad, CA: Hay House, 2003.

————, *Unplugged: Reclaiming Our Right to Die in America.* New York: AMACOM, 2006.

James Colgrove, *State of Immunity: The Politics of Vaccination in Twentieth-Century America.* Berkeley: University of California Press, 2007.

Jon B. Eisenberg, *Using Terri: The Religious Right's Conspiracy to Take Away Our Rights.* New York: HarperSanFrancisco, 2005.

Lawrence O. Gostin, *Public Health Law: Power, Duty, Restraint*, 2nd ed. Berkeley: University of California Press, 2008.

Bryan Hilliard, *The U.S. Supreme Court and Medical Ethics.* St. Paul, MN: Paragon House, 2004.

Stephen P. Kiernan, *Last Rights: Rescuing the End of Life from the Medical System.* New York: St. Martin's, 2007.

Jerry Menikoff, *Law and Bioethics: An Introduction.* Washington, DC: Georgetown University Press, 2002.

Grant H. Morris, *Refusing the Right to Refuse: Coerced Treatment of Mentally Disordered Persons*. Lake Mary, FL: Vandeplas, 2006.

Gregory Pence, *Medical Ethics: Accounts of the Cases that Shaped and Define Medical Ethics*. New York: McGraw Hill, 2007.

Ben A. Rich, *Strange Bedfellows: How Medical Jurisprudence Has Influenced Medical Ethics and Medical Practice*. New York: Springer, 2001.

Elyn R. Saks, *Refusing Care: Forced Treatment and the Rights of the Mentally Ill*. Chicago: University of Chicago Press, 2002.

Barry R. Schaller, *Understanding Bioethics and the Law: The Promises and Perils of the Brave New World*. Westport, CT: Praeger, 2007.

Udo Schuklenk, *Access to Experimental Drugs in Terminal Illness: Ethical Issues*. New York: Pharmaceutical Products Press, 1998.

Brette McWhorter Sember, *Gay & Lesbian Medical Rights*. Franklin Lakes, NJ: Career Press, 2007.

David N. Weisstub and Guillermo Díaz Pintos, eds., *Autonomy and Human Rights in Health Care*. New York: Springer, 2007.

Carl Wellman, *Medical Law and Moral Rights*. New York: Springer, 2005.

Bruce J. Winick, *The Right to Refuse Mental Health Treatment*. Washington, DC: American Psychological Association, 1997.

Sue Woodman, *Last Rights: The Struggle over the Right to Die*. Cambridge, MA: Da Capo Press, 2001.

Periodicals

George J. Annas, "Cancer and the Constitution—Choice at Life's End," *New England Journal of Medicine*, July 26, 2007.

———, "Forcible Medication for Courtroom Competence—The Case of Charles Sell," *New England Journal of Medicine*, May 27, 2004.

Paul S. Appelbaum, "Law & Psychiatry: Treating Incompetent Defendants: The Supreme Court's Decision Is a Tough *Sell*," *Psychiatric Services*, October 2003.

Robert Barnes, "Supreme Court Lets Stand Experimental-Drug Ruling," *Washington Post*, January 15, 2008.

Rebecca S. Barton, "Cruzan v. Director, Missouri Dept. of Health." *Issues in Law & Medicine*, Spring 1991.

Beryl Lieff Benderly, "Experimental Drugs on Trial," *Scientific American*, October 2007.

Debra A. Breneman, "Forcible Antipsychotic Medication and the Unfortunate Side Effects of *Sell v. United States*," *Harvard Journal of Law & Public Policy*, June 2004.

Scott Bullock, "Terminal Rights?" *Washington Times*, January 10, 2008.

Pete Busalacchi, "How Can They?" *Hastings Center Report*, September 1, 1990.

James Colgrove and Ronald Bayer, "Manifold Restraints: Liberty, Public Health, and the Legacy of *Jacobson v. Massachusetts*," *American Journal of Public Health*, April 2005.

Bette Jane Crigger, "The Court & Nancy Cruzan," *Hastings Center Report*, January 1, 1990.

Rebecca Dresser, "Investigational Drugs and the Constitution," *Hastings Center Report*, November/December 2006.

Daphne Eviatar, "If Sanity Is Forced on a Defendant, Who Is on Trial?" *New York Times*, June 21, 2003.

Sarah Fujiwara, "Is Mandatory Vaccination Legal in Time of Epidemic?" *Virtual Mentor*, April 2006.

Lawrence O. Gostin, "At Law: Compulsory Medical Treatment: The Limits of Bodily Integrity," *Hastings Center Report*, September/October, 2003.

———, "*Jacobson v Massachusetts* at 100 Years: Police Power and Civil Liberties in Tension," *American Journal of Public Health*, April 2005.

Linda Greenhouse, "Justices Restrict Forced Medication Preceding a Trial," *New York Times*, June 17, 2003.

———, "Supreme Court Limits Forced Medication of Some for Trial," *New York Times*, June 16, 2003.

Kerry Howley, "Dying for Lifesaving Drugs," *Reason*, August/September 2007.

Peter D. Jacobson and Wendy E. Parmet, "A New Era of Unapproved Drugs," *Journal of the American Medical Association*, January 10, 2007.

D. George Joseph, "Uses of *Jacobson v. Massachusetts* in the Age of Bioterror," *Journal of the American Medical Association*, November 5, 2003.

Charles Lane, "Court Sets Guidelines for Forced Medication," *Washington Post*, June 17, 2003.

———, "Justices Debate Medicating Mentally Ill Man for Trial," *Washington Post*, March 3, 2003.

William L. Leschensky, "Constitutional Protection of the 'Refusal-of-Treatment': Cruzan v. Director, Missouri Department of Health," *Harvard Journal of Law & Public Policy*, Winter 1991.

Duncan MacCourt and Alan A. Stone, "Caught in Limbo Between Law and Psychiatry," *Psychiatric Times*, June 2005.

Andrew H. Malcolm, "Nancy Cruzan: End to Long Goodbye," *New York Times*, December 29, 1990.

Hilde L. Nelson, "Cruzan Reconsidered," *Hastings Center Report*, January 1, 1991.

John Otrompke, "Court Deals Crippling Blow to FDA," *Life Extension Magazine*, September 2006.

Wendy E. Parmet, Richard A. Goodman, and Amy Farber, "Individual Rights versus the Public's Health—100 Years after *Jacobson v. Massachusetts*," *New England Journal of Medicine*, February 17, 2005.

Roger Pilon, "New Right to Life," *Wall Street Journal*, August 10, 2007.

Andrew Pollack, "Court Rejects Patient Right to Use Drugs Being Tested," *New York Times*, August 8, 2007.

Warren Richey, "To Stand Trial, Defendants Can Be Medicated by Force," *Christian Science Monitor*, June 17, 2003.

John A. Robertson, "Cruzan: No Rights Violated," *Hastings Center Report*, September 1, 1990.

Giles Scofield, "The Calculus of Consent," *Hastings Center Report*, January 1, 1990.

Alexandra M. Stewart, "Mandating HPV Vaccination—Private Rights, Public Good," *New England Journal of Medicine*, May 10, 2007.

Sherri Tenpenny, "Vaccinations and the Right to Refuse," *Whistleblower*, April 2007.

Ronald L. Trowbridge and Steven Walker, "The FDA's Deadly Track Record," *Wall Street Journal*, August 14, 2007.

Carolyn Tuft, "Judge Rejects Sell's Request for Trial," *St. Louis Dispatch*, November 22, 2004.

Angie A. Welborn, "Mandatory Vaccinations: Precedent and Current Laws," *CRS Report for Congress*, January 18, 2005.

Amy E. White, "Refusal of Treatment, Suicide Intervention and Autonomy," *Global Virtue Ethics Review*, April 1, 2004.

Susan M. Wolf, "Nancy Beth Cruzan: In No Voice at All," *The Hastings Center Report*, January 1, 1990.

Index

J

Jacobson, Henning
  arguments, 22, 25, 27–28, 35–37, 41, 48, 58
  case overview, 19–20
  court's rebuttals to arguments, 25–27, 28, 49, 59

Jacobson case. *See Henning Jacobson v. Commonwealth of Massachusetts* (1905)

John F. Kennedy Memorial Hosp. v. Heston, 81

Joint Commission on Accreditation of Health Care Organizations (JCAHO), 108

J.R., Parham v., 77

Judgments of patients' families, 77, 92, 99, 101

Judicial restraint, 186

Jurisdiction
  opined inappropriate, Supreme Court, 78, 79, 82–83, 122, 124, 161–162, 187–188
  questioned, Eighth Circuit, 116

K

Kennedy, Anthony, 129, 130
Kirby, United States v., 30
Kline, Natanson v., 88

L

Legislature, courts deferring to, 79, 161–162, 187–188

Liberalism and conservatism, in jurists, 186–188

Liberty for all, 22–23, 41

Liberty interest, 106, 126–127
  autonomy, 170–171
  bodily integrity, 128
  curtailed, 131–132

See also Fourteenth Amendment

Life-threatening situations, 155, 157–159

Lippmann, Stan, 32–39

Living wills, 70, 92–93, 108

Lochner v. New York, 34

Louisiana, Allgeyer v., 24

M

Madison, James, 187

Malloy, S. Elizabeth Wilborn, 104–109

Malpractice, 16

Mandatory vaccination. *See* Vaccination

Mariner, Wendy K., 46–56

Marketing, of harmful drugs, 177–182

Marshall, Thurgood, 17, 36, 107

Massachusetts, Snyder v., 88

Massachusetts state law, 19, 23–24, 29–30, 40–42

Medical rights, definition, 14

Medical technology and ethics
  drug development, 156, 167, 174–176, 177–182
  life-sustaining capabilities, 71, 85–86, 94, 101

Medications, purpose, 119–121
  See also Involuntary medicating; Refusing medication

Meekins, Tamar, 142, 146

Mentally ill defendants
  are not protected enough by *Sell* decision, 125–132, 142
  evaluation, 115, 134, 141, 143–144
  may disrupt trials per *Sell* ruling, 122–124